THE
TATRA
MOUNTAINS

THE
TATRA
MOUNTAINS

by

V. A. FIRSOFF

With 60 Illustrations

LINDSAY DRUMMOND
6 BUCKINGHAM ST.
W.C.2

DEDICATION

TO MY YOUNG BROTHER—FALLEN IN THE
UNARMED STRUGGLE FOR HUMAN DIGNITY,
WHO LOVED THE MOUNTAINS, FLOWERS
AND THE SKY OF THE TATRA.

NO ROLL OF HONOUR WILL CARRY
YOUR NAME—NO FLAGS WILL WAVE OVER
YOUR GRAVE.

MADE AND PRINTED IN GREAT BRITAIN

CONTENTS

ILLUSTRATIONS

* Negatives by J. Alan Cash.

* Negatives by J. Alan Cash.

PREFACE

THE TATRA MOUNTAINS, at least for natural beauty, are the pearl of Poland and Czechoslovakia, whose fate is so closely connected with the present world conflict. Both these countries played a prominent part in the events that led to the outbreak of the war, and both are yet destined to play perhaps as prominent a part at its close.

The Tatra is little known to the British public. There is, as far as I know, no book on the Tatra in the English language, and this alone should be a sufficient excuse for the publication of the present work.

I have lived in the Tatra many years and I love the place. To be sure, there are there no raw materials to produce munitions of war; but precisely because of this, I think it forms a fit subject for a book.

I think Ibsen in *Per Gynt* says that 'some need brandy, others need lies, and for the same reason we need fairy tales'. Dickens puts the same idea in a different form when he says that 'every man must have his romance'. Even Dr. Ley has recognised this principle in calling his grim organisation *Kraft durch Freude*.

Relaxation and escape from the reality of war are a necessity, and there can hardly be a better relaxation than travel in an unknown country. Mountains have been found to possess peculiar power of setting our minds free from daily troubles. So while real travel and mountaineering remain impracticable, let us enjoy them at least vicariously through description and photograph.

I should like to mention with gratitude the help and advice I have received from Dr. A. H. Kysucký in matters concerned with Slovakia, and Chapters X and XI of the book in particular, and to thank Dr. Adam Harasowski who has kindly supplied the music for two of the Tatra songs and the Polish and Czechoslovak Ministries of Information who have kindly provided some of the photographs.

Auchlean, 7th February, 1942.　　　　　V. A. FIRSOFF.

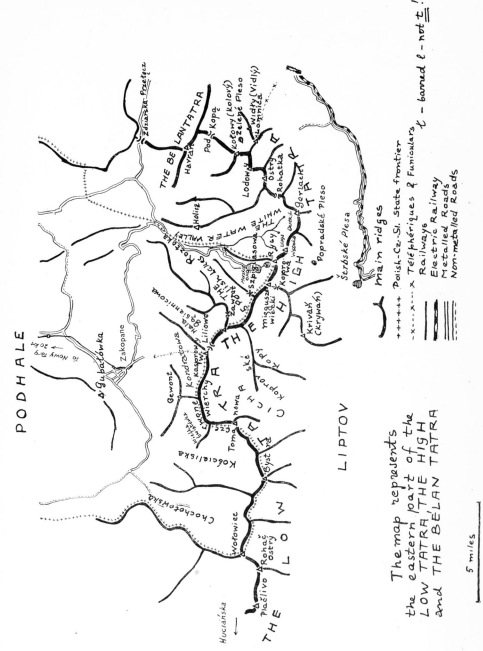

MAP OF THE TATRA MOUNTAINS

I

THE TATRA

'TATRA'—OR MORE CORRECTLY 'TATRY' originally meant
'waste'. High mountains, with a hard climate, a stony,
barren soil, a few pastures, lost among a sea of forest, roadless,
infested with wolves and bears, were little more to a peasant
than a waste, and that is what he called them. The meaning
of the word has since been lost, though some of the old
villagers use it to this day as a general noun. But the name
has remained, and the highest mountains of Poland and
Czechoslovakia are known as the Tatra or the Tatry,
the latter being the plural for Tatra. How this etymology is
supposed to account for the names of the two smaller mountain groups—the Matra and the Fatra in close vicinity is a
different question; yet there certainly must be a reason for
this.

On the old maps the region was represented by a vague and
arbitrary maze of peaks and streams, with a few bears, and spruce
trees to suggest dense forest and labelled as 'Montes Tartrae'.
This name has given rise to the association of the Tatra
with the Tartars; the 'Tartra' being conceived of as a sort of
Tartar Mountains. The association, however, is purely acci-
dental since at no known time have the Tartars ever been
there. When in the thirteenth century they actually invaded
Poland, took and burnt Cracow, north of the Tatra, and reached
as far as Silesia and Bohemia in the west, the sons of eastern
steppes shrank from contact with the mountains where there

would be no scope for their horses, and skirted the Tatra by nearly 100 miles.

Geographically the Tatra forms part of the vast mountain system of the Carpathians, extending all the way from Upper Silesia to the Iron Gate of the Danube, which divides them from the Balkan Mountains. But the Carpathians, though often extremely wild, are hardly Alpine in character. They seldom throw up naked rocks of any impressive bulk or gradient,* but undulate in round domes of grass and weathered stone; their form is Byzantine rather than Gothic.

The Tatra is different.

From Cracow the railway runs south through pleasant hilly country, but there is nothing in the landscape here to suggest the wild glory of the Tatra. Dark woods and cornfields follow each other, and almost imperceptibly a stern Scandinavian tone creeps into the scene. Clear mountain streams tinkle over rocky beds. Wooden cottages stand by scanty patches of tilled ground. Spruce forests crowd up to the railway track. The train slows down, climbs higher and higher; it struggles up to the main ridge of the Gorce,† puffing, out of breath. There it reaches the highest point and starts running stealthily—gradually increasing its speed, until it is racing toward Nowy Targ.‡ Suddenly the gates of the forest are thrown wide open—flat, ahead lies the sunlit plain of Podhale (Podhâlë), the Rocky Highlands. And far above the southern horizon, high, high in the sky among the wandering clouds, rise the blue shadows of jagged rocks with white streaks of snow—it is the Tatra.

The Tatra is barely thirty miles in length and hardly more than fifteen across—an island of rock and beauty.

In the north it is girded with a row of wooded hills which slope gently towards the Highlands of Poland. In the south the main

---

* Except perhaps some parts of the Transsylvanian Alps in Rumania.

† A mountain range of moderate altitude facing the Tatra some 30 miles farther north.

‡ A town about 20 miles north of the Tatra.

THE TATRA FROM THE SOUTH EAST

granite peaks rise sheer over the fertile Slovak valley of Liptov. Both sides have their distinct characteristics, and both have their full share of beauty.

The mountains, not unlike Cæsar's Gallia, consist of three parts.

The West or Low Tatra, of somewhat lower altitude than the central part, extends from the pass of Hucianska (930 m.) in the west to Liliowe (1954 m.) in the east and has the peak of Bystra (Rapid) of 8,600 feet for its highest point. It is largely Carpathian in character. Igneous rocks form the core of the system and appear uncovered in the peaks of the main range. But the foothills in the north are built of geologically young marls, slates and sandstones, while limestones and dolomites come to the surface higher up in the valleys. As the Tatra, however, is part of a broken surface fold, later sedimentary formations are often overtopped by a cap of hard gneiss or granite. Thus, the rocks of the summit offer greater resistance to erosion than do the mountainsides below, and this has resulted in the domelike but abruptly undercut shapes of the group of Czerwone Wierchy—or Red Peaks.

East of Liliowe and up to the pass of Pod Kopa (1756 m.) stretches the granitic High Tatra and still farther east lies the limestone group of the Belan Tatra, mostly grown over with grass, but of fairly steep gradient. Zdziarska Przelec—Zdiar Pass of 1,081 m. marks the eastern boundary of the Tatra.

The average altitude of the mountains is about 2,200 metres, or 7,000 feet, above sea level, but there are isolated peaks in the High Tatra which considerably exceed this figure. Gerlach

LIMESTONE CLIFFS OF THE
CZERWONE WIERCHY

IN THE HEART OF THE HIGH TATRA—
GANEK, WYSOKA AND GERLACH

measures fully 8,737 feet (2,663 m.) and Lomnica with its 8,642 feet (2,634 m.) had for a long time been considered as the highest summit of the group until more accurate measurements were made. Several other peaks are over 8,500 feet.

The High Tatra is steep and forbidding, more Alpine in parts than the Alps themselves. It is characterized by the strongly developed arêtes, the abruptness of the mountain faces and the relatively great height of the gaps and passes, most of which are difficult of access. But they are big mountains on a small scale—crowded, fragile and light, with dainty, turreted ridges, which would make most of the Alps look clumsy and somewhat crude by comparison.

The High Tatra occupies only about one-third of the small area of the Tatra, most of which lies west of Liliowe.* Yet what wealth of detail; peaks, valleys, lakes, waterfalls—all of them full of character and so different from one another. There are open, windy plateaux with small lakes lurking in the cavities among weathered boulders and dark wreaths of scrub-pine, plateaux surrounded at their edges with low, precipitous ridges, cutting like a knife into the blue of the sky or the grey of trailing cloud. There are terraced valleys rising in steps towards walls of stone which shoot up above the grey-green of debris and the white of summer snows like a smaller edition of the Grandes Jorasses. There are narrow, dead valleys where all is rock and silence and only here and there a meagre bunch of grass glitters in sunshine among the pitch-black, overhanging granites, and from time to time the breath of a distant waterfall or a squeak of an eagle is brought in by a gust of wind. There are lakes as deep as the sea and as smooth as a mirror. There is a wealth of wild flowers and the ever-changeable sky.

The Tatra is high enough to have full-size, regulation glaciers, and quite a few of its peaks rise above the line of eternal snow. But the precipitous faces and the narrow arêtes present too little opportunity for the snow to accumulate in large masses. So,

* *i.e.* belongs to the Low Tatra.

LIMESTONE ROCKS BLAZE IN SUNSHINE
AMONG THE DARK SILHOUETTES OF THE SPRUCES.

B

only hardened, white tongues survive throughout the summer in the narrow gullies of the High Tatra, particularly on the northern sides; and in places patches of ice linger near the summits. There are, however, at least two real glaciers, smallish things it is true, but quite unmistakable. The best known is that of the Miedziane Lawki (Copper Benches) in the north face of Lomnica. Although less than a thousand yards long, it is made of solid moving ice, with crevasses and ice grottoes. The other lies in the Snow Kettle in the rocks of Lodowy (2,630 m.), one of the highest peaks. 'Lodowy' or 'Ladovy' (in Slovak) means 'icy'—an appropriate name. But this baby-glacier is difficult of access, and has, therefore, escaped the wider publicity of the first; it contains considerably fewer tins and plum stones.

The limestone parts of the mountains abound in caves and grottoes, only partly explored, and every year brings new discoveries in the subterranean world. The most spectacular grottoes, over a mile in length, are the Belanské Kûpele in the Belan Tatra, on the Czechoslovak side.

The lower reaches of the Tatra valleys and the foothills are covered with spruce, silver fir, pine, larch and beech trees, some of them magnificent specimens with trunks many feet in girth. Not so very long ago the forest spread wide in all directions around the Tatra. It linked up in the north with the woods of the Gorce Mountains, and in the south the Nether Tatra, a parallel, lower mountain range on the other side of the Liptov Valley, stood out dark and forbidding among a sea of spruce and pine. Wild beasts and fierce robbers roamed those woods. The population was scant and nondescript. In the ninth century the Magyar hordes overran the Slovak lands in the south. They went pillaging and murdering throughout the rich Pannonian plains and the horror-stricken Slavs fled for refuge to the northern mountains. When in later years the Magyars settled down and founded the Kingdom of Hungary, the south slopes of the Tatra fell under its sway, while the north remained under the some-

DRAGON'S PEAK (SMOCZY SZCZYT)
FROM PATH TO RYSY

what shadowy rule of the Polish kings who sat on the Cracow throne.

But slowly man pushed nearer and nearer to the mountains. Already in the sixteenth century most of the now existing settlements of the Rocky Highlands received mention in legal documents. The towns of the fertile Liptov Valley had even achieved considerable prosperity long before that time. In 1412 the Hungarian King Sigismund of Luxemburg pawned to Poland 'the thirteen Spish townships', south of the Tatra, in return for the loan of 'threescore forty thousand Prague grosses'. The sum was never repaid and the thirteen townships were administered for 360 years by Polish 'starostas' (sheriffs), until in 1772 Austro-Hungarian troops of Empress Maria-Theresa marched in and occupied the district, without any opposition from the Poles. It was the first move in the First Partition of Poland. Soon after, the same year most of South Poland was likewise seized by the Austrians, and thus the Tatra fell under Habsburg domination. Spish (Zips) was incorporated in the Kingdom of Hungary, and the northern area became an Austrian domain as part of the new province of Galicia and Lodomeria.

But the people of the Tatra still lived much in the same old way, and the arm of the law and the human greed, which so often went with it, was too weak to impose serfdom on the Tatra freeholders. The wild forests were beyond the reach of the Austrian and Hungarian gendarmes, and the Tatra freebooters, of whom more later, were their real rulers.

The interest in the mountains for the mountains' sake did not come yet, and though the district was visited from time to time by bold travellers, they seldom ventured far into the Tatra, so that it remained all but unknown. One of the remarkable exceptions was an Englishman, Robert Townson, who in 1793 made the first fully authenticated ascent of Lomnica, then reputed to be the highest peak of the group.

For all this the Tatra for a thousand years had not known war. The occupation of 1772 was completed without fighting. And when the Habsburg Empire fell in 1918 and independent Poland and Czechoslovakia took its place on the Tatra slopes (the new frontier corresponding for the most part to that between Galicia and Hungary), the change ended in a few local disturbances, but was otherwise peaceful. It was Hitler's Germany that first brought the torch of war to the Tatra Mountains, when in September, 1939 the Alpine divisions of General List drove into Poland across their passes.

Such fighting as there had been before was limited to skirmishes between the Tatra freebooters and manor guards or gendarmes, and private 'misunderstandings' between noble families; the feudal castles and fortified residences scattered on the edges of the old forest land bear witness to the strifes and feuds of the past.

THE LOW TATRA IN AUTUMN

2

THE ROBBERS

IF THE ORDINARY PEASANT saw in the Tatra only a waste, a terrible desert in fact, with which it was better to have as little contact as possible, there were others who found a use for it. As we have already said, until about a hundred years ago the whole district, except for a few patches of pasture or cultivated ground, was one continuous forest. There were but scant and rough tracks, mainly left over by the Saxon miners who used at one time to work some silver, copper and iron mines in the mountains for the Polish kings. Later, however, the mines were exhausted and abandoned and the roads grew over with grass. The wild character of the mountains made them inaccessible according to the standards of the times.

Among these vast forests and mountain recesses found refuge all those who for some reason or other sought to escape the arm of the law, and particularly those independent spirits among the peasants who could not bear the burden of serfdom and preferred to live the life of outlaws.

> Drink, drink and go past Nowy Targ,
> Once you've passed it, you are safe

says an old song.

So, the tall, moss-grown spruces swayed in the wind and clouds raced across the Tatra as the robbers trod the forest way and sang their savage song of freedom,

I go to wealds!
Feather flutters in my hat.
I go to wealds!
Earth is rumbling as I step.
When I swing my faithful hatchet
Blood will splutter from the blow.
Where my axe will fall a-crashing
Hot, red blood will pour in streams.

The night is dark!
There's a glow among the trees.
The night is dark!
Does the evil evil woo?
In the glade between the spruces
'Vatra's'* burning in the weald.
Are the forest wives a-warming?
Do the devils lead the dance?

Hey, brother young!
Come and join the jolly band!
Hey, brother young!
Come and join the jolly band!
If the fates should turn against you,
On the gibbet you will swing,
Or doubloons and silver thalars
You will shower on your way. . . . †

Apart from the outlaws of all classes, among whom were not a
few Polish nobles as well, the Tatra had its own population which
lived in rather primitive conditions and until relatively recent
times remained pagan. Its history and origin are matters of conjecture ; this has probably given rise to the idea, at present

* 'Vatra'—a Tatra name for fire (see Chapt. III).

† This is only part of the "Robbers' March". The original is rhymed, but
here as well as in other songs rhyme has been sacrificed for character. For
music, see page 43.

23

officially adopted by the Nazis, that the people of the Tatra were one of the 'lost German tribes'—the Marcomanni. There is, however, no conceivable evidence to support this view, which may be brushed lightly aside as one of the minor German brain-waves. In fact, it is completely absurd and it seems fairly probable that the scarce pastoral population of the Tatra was of Rumanian origin. So at least certain linguistic affinities would indicate, although, there may have been Saxon miners or Zipser* Germans among the Robbers.

Sheep supplied the main wealth for this population, though some other forms of farming were practised on a very modest scale—as far as the short summer and the poor soil allowed.

The swelling ranks of the outlaws gradually absorbed the local population, forming what might almost be described as a new race. They, though largely living the peasants' life, could not make much of a living out of their peaceful occupations and sought other sources of income. Their eyes began to turn to the rich Slovak and Hungarian plains to the south of their mountains. Bands of resolute and fierce Tatra Highlanders would suddenly descend on some Hungarian manor, convent or a small settlement, sack it and escape back to their mountain fastnesses, beyond the reach of Austro-Hungarian gendarmes. The Tatra Robbers cherished a strong feeling against the rich and powerful as the natural outcome of their personal past and such traditions as had been inherited from their predecessors, but in their forays they did no harm to the poor and simple. In fact, tradition would have it that they often helped them out with their spoils.

The Robbers have thus become a symbol of freedom—something in the style of Robin Hood—more particularly they were fighters against the serfdom enforced at that time on the peasantry of the surrounding districts. There were some famous Robber Chiefs, like the semi-legendary Janosik,† the scourge of the rich

* Zips is a district with a German minority south of the Tatra.

† Janosik's nationality is a matter of conjecture. He was probably a Slovak but he is the national hero of both the Polish Uplands and Slovakia.

VIEW TOWARDS THE IRON GATE ACROSS POPRADSKÉ PLESO

and the protector of the poor, around whose personality many legends are centred and whose exploits supply motives for popular song.

Janosik is said to have been noble and fearless. His fame had reached as far as Vienna and his name struck terror into the hearts of Hungarian magnates. An obviously untrue legend says that the Empress Maria-Theresa of Austria (called somewhat affectionately Tereska by the people of the Tatra) took a fancy to the Robber Chief and on one occasion danced with him. But a woman brought about his downfall. His girl, mad with jealousy, betrayed Janosik to the Imperial gendarmes. She had scattered dry peas on the floor of the room where he lay asleep, and as he jumped on his 'level feet' to defend himself, he slipped and fell. So, he was overpowered, brought to the Orava Castle, and hung there by the 'middle rib' to force him to give away his comrades. According to the current Slovak version of the story, he refused stubbornly, and managed to escape, but was caught again, sentenced to death and hanged.

There are many legends of his exploits and his death and often they contradict one another. In fact, it is possible that several personalities have been mixed up in the legend. This is all the more probable since Janošík is only a Christian name (Johnny), so that there may have been more than one Robber Chief who were so called.

The Slovak tradition gives the Liptov town of Svatý Mikuláš as the place of his execution, and it appears to be right, as documents have been found recording a death sentence carried out there in 1713 on a young robber, Janosik by name. But the traditional Gural 'mourning tune' *When Janosik Was Led to Levoča* would have that place as the end of his journey. It tells how the great and noble Robber Chief Janosik—the King of the Tatra—was brought to Levoča under a powerful escort, and recounts the scenes of his trial and death. The noble Hungarian lords had come down to Levoča to see him die, and Janosik, condemned to death, turned to them and said,

> Hey, you, Lords of Liptov,
> Let Janosik dance once more!

'But they didn't let him dance,'—the story goes on—'for they feared him still.' So, Janosik renewed his last request for the second and the third time, and at the third time it was granted by the Liptov Lords, 'for they feared him no more'. A band played to him, and Janosik danced 'small stepping beautifully, with his darling Death at his side'.

The Robbers were proud independent people, with an interesting local culture, and they recognized no authority. Although to-day there are no more robbers in the Tatra, much of their old spirit survives.

> High lords you, high lords you,
> And lords you will remain.
> But never will you, oh, never
> Be lords over us here.

is a Tatra song. . . . I remember a train puffing heavily up the steep rise before Zakopane, the mountain resort and the capital of the Tatra uplands. Two local lads in their colourful white trousers of thick, heavy wool with red-and-blue embroideries, and short, embroidered, sleeveless sheepskin jackets, were singing blissfully at the top of their voices a local tune—and they do go up to a high pitch when they sing.

Suddenly a very high police officer emerged from the next compartment and turned on them roughly, demanding that they should stop singing at once. They looked down at him disdainfully, their eyes blazing with anger, and said both together:

'And who are you to talk like that? People here don't object to our singing, do they? So what have *you* got to say? We are free and there's no harm in singing'.

'You had better keep quiet'—added another—'or you might find yourself on the other side of the window before you know what's happened.'

27

The police officer, used to tame obedience, disappeared from the scene rather sheepishly.

It must be known that the Tatra Highlanders are proud of their singing and a derogatory remark on that subject is a mortal insult. But in defence of the police officer I am inclined to admit that the charm of the performance is not always unalloyed. Anyhow, the alleged Marcomanni seem signally ill-adapted to the Nazi ideology, and it appears that from time to time a missing Nazi is found by smell in some lonely place among the mountains.

3

TAKE IT EASY

THOSE PEOPLE OF THE TATRA, who live in the uplands parts north of the mountain chain, known as the Rocky Highlands, speak a dialect of Polish frequently difficult for a Pole from the plains to understand. The southern slopes of the mountains are inhabited by Slovaks, though no definite boundary separates them from the Poles and both these closely related races merge into one another imperceptibly. The Highlanders, or 'Gurale' (plural form of the singular 'Gural'), as they are called in Polish, have quite a few words of their own. Thus, instead of using the Polish word *ogień* (Latin *ignis*, Engl. 'ignite') for fire, they prefer an odd Sanskrit term *vatra*, and there are many other words in the dialect which are common to the mountain tribes of both Europe and Asia. One would, however, look in vain for any traces of Marcomannic influences, unless we choose to regard as such *swarc* (*shvarts*) used for boot-polish or *fajerman*, pronounced as the English word 'fireman' and having the same meaning. The obvious historical origin of these words hardly needs stressing. Incidentally, I have even met a Gural who used the words 'horse' and 'spring' in their normal Anglo-Saxon meaning. But it transpired that he had lived in America, where he had been working in the coal-mines. 'I had to leave there',—he explained—'because the water from those Lakes was bad for my health. . . .'.

They are slow speakers, as becomes free men, and there is a slow dignity in their behaviour. They also have a keen and ready sense of humour.

Weather in the Tatra is one of the commonest topics of conversation. It is changeable, freakish and unreliable, far more so than in England, whose climate has been so unjustly reviled.

Near the entrance to the railway station of Zakopane stands a row of horse-cabs, with cabmen drowsing lazily inside, while a persistent drizzle is drumming on the cab roofs, which are all up. The sky is overcast and the clouds cut off the sight of the mountains. In fact, the scene looks like a dismal plain.

A new holiday-maker, a lady, is fidgeting uneasily with her umbrella, trying to rouse one of the cabmen from indifference.

'Gazda!' she calls. It means 'landlord': you couldn't possibly address a real Gural in white trousers (rather more often grey than pure white) in any other manner.

The gazda doesn't budge. But finally he responds and not he alone. There is a commotion and several cabmen gather around the prospective customer, each trying to win her for himself.

'Look at his horse! It wouldn't walk a mile', says one of them. But he is too late; our gazda has already seated his passenger safely inside his cab and drives off at a breakneck pace to prove that his horse is a regular racer.

But the lady is not satisfied. She is looking anxiously around for some sign of the mountains—in vain.

'Tell me, gazda', she asks in the end 'does it always rain like that here?'

'Oh no, lady. It doesn't. Sometimes it snows as well.'

An old gazda stands leaning on his scythe at the edge of a small meadow scanning his poor crop of grass. I am passing by.

'God bring luck!' I venture.

'God give,' he answers gravely, as prescribed by the ritual.

'And what do you think of the weather?' I ask the perennial question.

He pauses thoughtfully and consults the sky with feathery postföhn clouds.

OLD CHALETS NEAR ZAKOPANE

'Oh, it will be fine. Oh, it will be. . . . Sure. . . . Unless it pours', he answers with deliberation, a merry twinkle in his eye.

The robbers had left many treasures, hidden in their mountain haunts: golden ducats and silver thalars, gems and arms—some real, some imaginary. But at the time when Zakopane was 'discovered' by Dr. Chalubiński in the second half of the last century, and gradually came to be a mountain resort, there were few robbers alive and they were ancients who neither could nor would wield their hatchet-sticks for loot. Soon after they died out completely and nothing but memory, songs, dances and quaint glass paintings remained of the 'good old times'. And there were, of course, the treasures, concealed deep in the grottoes of the Tatra, under huge boulders or in old hollow trees.

Where there are treasures, there must also be secret codes and signs leading to them, and treasure-hunters attempting to ferret them out, and the Tatra was no exception to the rule. Some treasures had even actually been found, while the search for others gave pleasant thrills and expectations to those who felt so disposed.

One of such treasures, a large one, was said to have been re-posing for a good hundred years beneath a huge stone on the summit of a smallish mountain called the Great Lubań. There were marks in plenty and stories to match which all served to show that that was *the* place. But the slopes of the Great Lubań were steep and the stone was very heavy. Some of the heftiest lads from the surrounding villages—and the Gurals are a fine, long-limbed, tall race—gathered on the summit on several occasions and tried to heave the stone. Yet each time they failed. Finally, they succeeded, with much shouting and wiping off the sweat from their brows, in bringing up to the very top a team of horses.

Ropes were fixed round the stone and after more shouting, pushing and pulling, the rock rolled over on to its side.

No treasure, however, was found underneath. Instead, on the

reverse of the stone there stood scraped out in big, awkward letters the following sentence:

THANK YOU KINDLY FOR TURNING ME
OVER, FOR MY SIDE HAS GOT NUMB.

It was a tremendous practical joke of an amazingly old vintage. Generations of robbers must have laughed themselves hoarse with it, but they had kept the secret.

ZAKOPANE SLEDGES CAN GO ALMOST ANYWHERE

4

LOCAL COLOUR

OLD NATIONAL COSTUMES, once worn in the countries of
Europe, are rapidly disappearing, and in many countries
they have passed altogether from human memory. But the Tatra
Highlander is as proud of his white woollen trousers as a
Scottish Highlander is of his kilt, and they cling to their old
traditional ways.

He may be very poor, but if he wears his trousers, which were
once white, with some traces of old embroideries on them, he
can still enjoy the right to self-respect and a measure of considera-
tion from the others. Dare he, however, appear in ordinary
townsman's clothes in a similarly dilapidated state, he would be
just a 'lowland sansculotte' (*ceper przez portków*) and feel quite
uncomfortable in a Gural village.

So, a man's traditional costume consists, in the first place, of
these trousers made with very thick and solid white wool and
sitting tightly on the legs. A stripe of blue wool, about an inch
broad, runs all along the outer side of the trouser leg and there
are two red tufts, one at the ankle and another at the end of a
flap covering the instep. On the front part over the thighs, large
ornamental 'parzenicas' (*pâzheneetsa*) in bright red and blue,
complete the effect.

The trousers are supported by a leather belt. 'Full dress' in-
cludes a peculiar belt, some 10–15 ins. wide on the front, though
much narrower at the back, and richly studded with brass tacks.
Tatra robbers carried pistols and daggers behind such belts,

GURAL DANCERS

A STREET SCENE IN A GURAL VILLAGE

which were probably meant also as armour to protect the most vulnerable part of the body. At present they are worn only on rare occasions, except by head shepherds on the Alm who use them as a mark of their rank.

The shirt in olden times used to be boiled in butter to make it waterproof and it was black. Nowadays, however, only ordinary white shirts are in general use. A sheep-skin jerkin, with or without sleeves, mostly embroidered with red, blue and green wool or silk, though sometimes plain, is worn for everyday use, except in hot weather, by men and women alike. The 'cuha' (pr. tsuho), a sort of loose, collarless jacket of white wool, similar to that used for trousers, with green and red embroideries, is donned on ceremonial occasions. Its sleeves are not made use of and it rests easily on the shoulders, supported on the chest by a silk band of vivid colour (mostly red), or a strap adorned with brass brooches, which holds the two sides together.

The hat is small and round; it is made of hard black (originally brown) felt, and is decorated with a band of white mussel-shells. The Tatra robbers in old paintings appear in tall red hats. But these seem to have been only a ceremonial headwear; for ordinary purposes hats similar to those now in use have been worn by both robbers and peasants, if indeed any strict discrimination between them could be made, for centuries past. Sometimes an eagle feather is stuck on the left behind the string of mussel-shells.

This national attire would not be complete without a peculiar walking stick with a small steel, or sometimes brass, hatchet for the hand grip. It is a walking stick, a useful tool and also a weapon at times. The robbers wielded it as a sort of battle-axe. But even now village lads do occasionally stage up a fight over a girl, or some other mortal offence, with their hatchet sticks. Mostly it ends with a few blows, parried by the opponent. A popular ditty runs,

Hey, far beyond the mountains, beyond the woods,

Two Highlanders started a fight with their hatchets.
Hey, lads, do stop fighting! Make up your quarrel!
Look at the girl's two long pigtails;
Go on, divide between you Mary's fine, dark hair!

But this advice is not always followed and some fights are apt to prove fatal for one—or even both sides, since the Gurals are fearless and fierce fighters and take their quarrels seriously.

A woman's dress is less elaborate, and certainly less local in style, for it has been very much influenced by Cracow patterns. Certainly the sheep-skin jerkin is local. So, also, are the attractive sandals of pleated leather, strapped up the ankle, and studded with brass tacks. These are also worn by men, though in general they content themselves with ordinary shoes, ski boots or nailed climbing boots. Leather-soled, felt slippers, decorated with bright colours, are another variation of local feminine foot-wear.

Otherwise, both the gazda's wife and daughters wear wide skirts, mainly dark green with red flowers, though orange and red skirts with blue or green flowers are not infrequent. A coloured bandana serves as head cover. Young women like to add to their graces by heavy strings of red corals falling loosely on their lap from their neck. But all this, and also the short,

GURAL TYPES

black sash, adorned with embroideries and beads and braced with a red tape on the breast, comes from the district of Cracow, some eighty miles farther north, and can hardly be considered as really and truly Gural.

In any case, a Sunday crowd on the way to or from church makes a brightly coloured picture. The sheep-skin jerkins, however, have one unpleasant characteristic, especially when new—they smell quite a bit and the smell couldn't be described as particularly attractive.

5

FOLK DANCES

THE FUNDAMENTAL MOTIVE of the Gural dance is, as in most folk dances, the wooing of the girl by the boy. As may be expected of a manly and warlike race, the boy finds the way to her heart by showing to the best advantage his strength and nimbleness. But this is not enough ; he must also please her by his song and a display of ready wit.

This conception makes the girl's part largely passive and in any case—secondary. In the two of the local dances: the 'drobny' which may be translated as 'small-step', and the 'krzesany' (kshesani), a name difficult to render in English, but whose approximate meaning is 'whetted' or 'hewn', she flees seductively from her pursuing partner, with her hands poised on her hips. In the 'Robbers' Dance, 'zbójnicki' (zbooinitskee) —men perform alone. It was originally danced around a bonfire, the dancers facing each other and beating the rhythm on the ground with the hatchets of their sticks. The figures of this dance are somewhat similar to the 'Cossack', but differently timed, and one of them, as can be seen on old glass paintings, was a jump across the fire. It was the highest achievement, as the paintings indicate, simultaneously to drain a bottle of wine with one hand, and press the trigger of a pistol with the other.

Since, however, the Robbers passed away, no living man seems to have performed the trick. . . . Good old times!

In the remaining dances there are only two dancers, a girl and a boy on the floor, while the others await their turn—so at least they are supposed to do, if they respect tradition.

Two or three-stringed fiddles and a bass make the band. The bass is usually small, like a 'cello, and is carried by the musician at his belt. Double basses are allowed occasionally. The fiddler, when playing, doesn't hold the fiddle against his shoulder, but props it against his left chest, beating time with his right foot on the floor. And so the dance goes on.

The lad, before beginning the dance, steps out to the middle of the floor, faces the orchestra and sings the tune he wants to be played. All dance tunes are also songs, most of them traditional, though existing in many variations. But the tortuous way to the heart of the beloved is much more thorny than that. To be really smart he has to improvise words to the traditional tune and to make them as funny and topical as he can contrive.

The performance over, he puts a tip into the bass. This is an old custom, and once Janosik used to shower into it silver thalars and golden coins with a generous hand. It was then that

> The freebooters come to dance
> To a cellar all of stone
> And they bid the players play
> And watch as their feet go round!   Hey!
>
> Oh, I should be glad to dance,
> If my legs were not so crook'd.
> But the crooked legs I've got,
> Up I jump and down they bend!   Hey!*

as the situation was summed up by somebody with a sense of humour and crooked legs. This is a Robbers' Dance which is certainly an extremely strenuous exercise, and requires 'legs as if of steel or by devils given'—no chance for crooked ones.

The Tatra Highlanders are fond of music and Janosik's example forbids meanness towards the bass, which makes playing a profitable and respectable profession. The instruments and the

* For Music, see p. 43.

40

tunes are passed from father to son and there are families who have played for many generations, extending back to Janosik himself, and perhaps to still older times.

The bagpipe called 'kobza', used to be a popular instrument and the Tatra robbers were accompanied on their expeditions by bag-pipers as well as fiddlers who played for them their favourite tunes. But nowadays it is scarce and most bagpipe players are old men. The name 'kobza' or 'koza' means 'she-goat'; it comes from the small wooden head of a mountain goat with which Gural bagpipes are adorned at the top.

The Gural music differs considerably, in spirit and form, from the Polish lowland melodies. Though all Gural dances are also songs, the reverse is not true, and there are quite a few tunes un-connected with dancing. Local melodies are usually subdivided, apart from the already mentioned dances, into marches (which are not danced), wedding tunes and the so-called 'Highland' ('wierchowa') and 'slow' ('ozwodna') tunes which serve to open the dance and give the party an opportunity to warm up to the coming quick movements by the slower-timed 'Gural Dance', forming the choregraphic equivalent of these 'times'. All these tunes may be either traditional—'old-worldly', as they are called —or 'new', the genuine Robbers songs and dances and the com-positions of the older local musicians, such as Sabala or Obrochta, being classed in the first category.

The musical phrase and period show some interesting features. Thus, in the 'slow' ('ozwodna') tunes we meet almost exclusively with the five-bar phrase, subdivided into two parts of three and two bars respectively. To this is added a five-bar sequel, which gives a ten-bar period, a form extremely rare in folk music. In the 'hewn' and 'smallstep' dances the period of two four-bar phrases is the prevailing pattern. In many melodies the whole is extended to several five- or four-bar periods through the addition of variants.

The harmonization is hard; the style of the melodies is stern and primitive, but natural and spontaneous in expression. Among intervals we find in the upper parts the very characteristic augmented fourths; and perfect fifths and thirds in the middle register; while perfect octaves, fourths and fifths are the rule in the bass. Syncopation, both symmetrical and assymmetrical, is an outstanding rhythmical characteristic, and the accentuation of certain beats gives special prominence to the rhythm of the Gural tunes. Appoggiaturas are frequent in the upper parts, but there are no trills.

The sound of Gural music, based as it is on an especial tonality, is not always pleasant to an unaccustomed ear, used to the normal tonal system. But its originality and spontaneity will appeal to any one with wider musical interests.

The Tatra has exercised a great influence on Polish art in general and on music in particular. But most of the earlier works, connected with the Tatra, though their inspiration was undoubtedly due to experiences of the mountain scenery and even Gural legends, stood in no direct relation to the local tunes. 'The Tatra Album' by I. J. Paderewski, supplied the first notable exception to this rule and was based on the popular Tatra melodies, played to the famous pianist by the local bard Bartek Obrochta* and his Gural orchestra. Among the outstanding Polish composers whose names are connected with the Tatra was Mieczyslaw Karlowicz, a great lover of these mountains where he found a rich source of musical ideas. He was killed by an avalanche in 1909 when ski-ing in the Tatra. But it was left to Karol Szymanowski to appreciate in full the riches of the Tatra folklore. He spent many years in Zakopane, where he died in 1937, studying the old robber songs on which much of his own music was based. One of his disciples, Maklakiewicz undertook the tremendous work of writing down all the most important traditional Gural tunes, transmitted from generation to generation but never recorded before, and published these under the title *Muzyka Podhala* (The Music of Podhale).

* Obrochta, as a young juhas, used to play to the last Tatra robber chief, Wojtek Mateja, who took a fancy to him, and on several occasions he accompanied his band on its southern forays.

1.   "The Robbers' Song of Freedom" (p. 23).
2.   "The Freebooters came to Dance" (p. 40).

6

ZAKOPANE AND PROGRESS

Z AKOPANE, which literally means a place beyond the tilled
ground—'Za-kopane'—'Beyond—tilled (dug)'* is first
mentioned in a legal document dated 1630. It was the robbers'
headquarters, sheltered among the spruce and beech forest at
the foot of the Tatra. Only a few bad roads led there, and quiet
folk of honest calling did not venture that way without appre-
hension.

But, as already said, it was 'discovered' in the second half of
the last century by one Dr. Tytus Chalubiński, who in the
company of his friend, a local bard Sabala, some 'cepry' (or
people of the plains) and an army of guides began cumbersome
peregrinations through the trackless mountains of Tatra, exposed
to the chills of night and thrills of exploration. The mountains
were wild, virgin for all but shepherds and their flocks and
simply swarming with legends and songs. And so Chalubiński
and his freinds would spend their rest time, when it was fine,
sitting on boulders or logs in front of a glittering 'vatra' under
the canopy of spruce branches and a starry sky, singing and playing, and drinking tea or coffee.

His example was contagious and from these modest beginnings
developed the local variety of Alpinism, since then given the
name of Tatrism. Zakopane, whose air was found to possess

* There exists a different though less probable explanation of the name,
which can also mean 'buried'. It is said that the legendary founder of the place
buried there a few seeds of corn for trial.

THE VALLEY OF ZAKOPANE AND
THE TATRA FROM GUBALÓWKA

curative properties for the diseases of the lungs, slowly became a mountain resort, and in 1874 the Polish Tatra Society was founded, which began opening and maintaining popular tracks, building tourist huts and performing similar useful services.

Zakopane grew. Houses in the local style cropped up in democratic disorder along the surrounding roads, where mud in rainy weather was as deep as the stony ground would permit. But the nearest railhead was still some forty miles by road—and a dubious one at that—and there was no other means of communication except a hay-cart which was both slow and jerky, though very romantic!

Later on, there came a ramshackle railway and a couple of metalled roads in continuous repair, not unlike some London streets in peacetime. A gradual orgy of improvement had set in, which culminated shortly before the war in the construction of a téléférique, a cable-railway and a sledge-hoist for impatient skiers, not to mention a galaxy of bigger and smaller hotels and the new unfinished 'Autobahn', the work on which is apparently being carried on under the present regime.

Thus, Zakopane has become a fairly modern place of nearly thirty thousand inhabitants, with shops, cinemas, cafés, restaurants, sanitoria where the consumptive can pass their time in comfort hoping for recovery, a ski and an ice-hockey stadium, a hot-spring swimming pool, sun-bathing grounds and similar facilities for those who have time and money and care for such things. Bathrooms, however, are still somewhat scarce, except in bigger 'pensions', and it is maintained by some visitors that local landladies are addicted to the heinous practice of drying up old tea leaves in the sun and using them once again for the benefit of their customers. This is probably unfounded and malicious gossip. At any rate for the time being, they haven't any real tea.

In winter there are skiers and mutually hostile ski schools, some tobogganing and a bob-sleigh course, though it is not too grand if compared with the paragons of its kind. When later

ZAKOPANE LIES IN A SHELTERED VALLEY BETWEEN THE
MAIN RANGE AND THE WOODED HILL OF GUBALÓWKA

hours bring rest upon the toiling earth, there is dancing and bridge-playing in places devised for the purpose. And, above all, whatever the time of the day or night, there is the Tatra—all in white!

Zakopane, despite all its modernities (some of them quite sufficiently horrid), is an old place and that gives it character, which local residents seem often to forget. It is still half-village-half-town, with large empty spaces, wooden cottages with steep roofs and walls built of heavy beams, the slots between which are stuffed with pleated wood-shavings or, when the house is very old, with moss. This distinguishes the place from the smaller and neater, but rather nouveau-riche, fashionable resorts on the Czecho-Slovak side of the mountains.

Outlying hamlets in the neighbourhood of Zakopane still remain practically untouched by modern civilization, and people there have escaped many of its shadier aspects, so often apparent among the populations of tourist resorts. They are nicer there— just as they have been described by the Polish writer Kazimierz Tetmajer in his cycle of short stories *In the Rocky Highlands*. They can still say like the Finns,

> Our land is poor, so it shall be
> To them who thirst for gold. . . .

One foggy day in the West Tatra, as I was carrying myself moodily up a grassy slope, with the wind shivering on the boulders and glittering spray settling on my waterproofs, I met an old Highlander, one of those who used to be—with long straw and silver hair, combed down straight.

'Praised be Jesus Christ', he said.

'For the centuries of centuries, Amen', I answered.

This formality over, the old man shook his head and asked, 'And where are you going like that?'

'Up!' I retorted curtly, beckoning to the invisible summit.

'Oh, you would', he said thoughtfully after a becoming

silence. 'Why, wouldn't you come down to my hut? It isn't much to mention. But it's a cold day and you can warm yourself a bit and have a hot drink of milk.'

I thanked him and followed him to his little chalet with a roof weighted with stones against the foehn. We sat and had a chat about how the world was going on, the weather and things. The old man nodded, made little witty remarks and again relapsed into the thoughtful silence of an Indian chieftain. But money for his milk he refused with indignation.

'Do come again when you are here', he said as we parted. 'It's lonely up here for an old man like me.'

I promised I would, but I have never been there since.

FRESH SNOW IN THE FIVE POLISH LAKES

7

THE 'WHITE' ROOM AND THE 'BLACK' ROOM

THE ROCKY HIGHLANDS have no sand or chalk to make mortar with, but wood and stone are found in plenty, and these are the two kinds of material at the disposal of a local builder. Stone, however, is hard and difficult to handle. Moreover, as he has no mortar, he can't use stone to build real, solid walls. Accordingly stone is used only for foundations; all the rest of the house is made of wood.

It was difficult in old times to obtain iron tools. Even nails were scarce. So everything possible had to be made of native wood, which was close at hand and cost nothing except the trouble of preparing it and fetching it to the building site. This has exercised a powerful influence on the development of the local style.

A typical Gural cottage is built with tree trunks, stripped of their bark and slightly squared at their sides with an axe. The ends of the trunks are strutted so as to fit into one another where the walls intersect, thus forming a firm structure. These intercrossed ends protrude beyond the wall for some ten inches or more and are very characteristic. The roof is built at a steep angle to prevent the accumulation of the snow and extends about two yards beyond the wall (okap) to protect the windows from rain and snow. It is covered with shingles.

The width of the beams of which the house is built is the object of the gazda's pride, and the fewer used to make a wall,

VILLAGE CHURCH IN KOŚCIELISKO NEAR ZAKOPANE
(ZAKOPANE STYLE)

VILLA IN ZAKOPANE STYLE BUILT BY S. WITKIEWICZ

the more satisfied he feels. When the beams are dry, slots between them are stuffed with moss, though nowadays wood-shavings woven into a sort of pigtail are substituted. These have to be examined from time to time and given an additional push, for they often get loosened or are completely blown out by the wind. They have, however, this advantage that they do not absorb moisture as moss would.

In the centre of the house there is a spacious door, adorned with a pattern of wooden pegs; it opens into a sort of hall with a staircase or—more modestly—a ladder leading to the garret where hay, tools, reserve garments and suchlike are stored and where in rainy weather the gazda's wife hangs her washing. The hall itself is not inhabited, but it has two doors. The right door opens into the 'black room' and the left into the 'white room'.

The difference between the two rooms, which are of equal size, is that the 'black' one is the living room proper. Here the whole family spend most of their time in winter, sleep and have their meals. In one corner—the inside left—is a kitchen stove with an oven where bread is baked. A long bench goes all round the wall; and parallel to it at a man's height runs a shelf. Below the back wall are the beds and above these—on the shelf, are holy pictures painted on glass and others representing dancing robbers and similar conventional scenes. Nowadays these pictures are often replaced by cheap lithographs. The furniture consists of a table, some chairs and stools and a heavy ornamental chest with clothing and other important possessions. Dressers with plates, cups, a few jars, etc., and spoon-racks with spoons, complete the traditional picture.

The 'white room' is used only on solemn occasions or by guests. It has no stove, but its furniture is similar to that of the 'black room', though of a finer finish.

The ceiling, made of clean-polished wooden boards, rests on two, three or more transversal beams and these in turn are supported by one big beam, running the length of the room. This beam, called 'sosreb' (pr. sosremb), is marked in the middle

INSIDE A GURAL COTTAGE

with a cross and the year of construction, two figures on each side of the cross. It is also richly decorated with carvings.

In old times the fire-place in the 'black room' had no chimney and the smoke escaped through an opening in the ceiling to the garret where cheeses, meat and, occasionally, sausages were smoked. After a few years the walls and the ceiling above the stove would become completely black, which has given the 'black room' its name.

Such houses are still to be found here and there, especially in the villages remote from the main lines of communication and the novelties they bring. But they are becoming scarce.

In the western part of the Highlands, called Orava, houses are bigger and have two stories, the rooms of the first floor being accessible by means of a staircase and a gallery running all along the front wall. The generous proportions of the 'black room' are indicated by the old prescription that it should be possible to turn round a cart with two horses inside it. Only rich gazdas, however, could afford to carry out this prescription to the letter. The floor of an Orava 'black room' is made of beaten clay. Orava cottages have no halls, and their 'black' and 'white' rooms are contiguous.

In the second half of the last century a Polish architect Stanislaw Witkiewicz developed the so-called Zakopane style, based on the traditional Gural building art, but somewhat more sophisticated. Most of the older and many of the new wooden and even brick buildings of Zakopane follow this style, though lately a whole mass of horrible outcrop of so-called 'modernity' has done much to spoil the character of the place.

Local wooden churches, some of them two and more centuries old, are of considerable interest. In ecclesiastic architecture, village builders strove to imitate in wood the stone and brick Gothic churches they had seen in towns. They had, however, to rely on their own experience and often introduced various features of the local style, such as steep roofs covered with shingles and protruding beyond the walls, or carved beams to support the rafters

54

of the nave. No genuine local style of church architecture has been evolved, but the effect of the blend is extremely characteristic and generally pleasing to the eye. The mixture of Gural wood motives, decorated with bright colours, with the austere granite Gothic of the main Zakopane church is less happy. But a similar combination of wood and stone without colours, as represented by the tourist hotel in Hala Gasiennicowa (Gongsienitsova), may be quite pleasant.

8

'SUDDEN CROSS' AND SORROWING CHRIST

T HE GURALS have in their fingers an itch for wood carving, and soft fir wood lends itself excellently to the purpose.

One of the most frequent traditional motives in their orna-
ments is the 'sudden cross'. The 'sudden cross' is our old ac-
quaintance—it can hardly be called a friend—the Swastika! It is
historically associated with the cult of the sun and fire, mankind's
oldest religion, and is a conventional symbol of the former. As
such the swastika is common to many races of Europe and Asia,
not necessarily only Aryan. Another decorative motive connected with the ancient cult is a circle divided into six parts by
an intersecting arch of the same radius—often with 'beams'
radiating from it. It is particularly frequent on the doors.
(See p. 53).

The 'sudden cross', a Christianized relic of the pagan past, was
meant to be a charm keeping away all sort of "suddennes",
including sudden death and similar blitzkriegs. The Gural
swastika, however, for the most part faces the opposite way to
the Nazi Hackenkreuz and stands flat on its side. Sometimes it
assumes not easily recognizable forms, degenerating to a round
mark surrounded by what could be described as four flames
spurting out of it, carved out with a sharp object in wood. But
it is always the 'sudden cross' and there is no mistake about it.

Other favourite ornamental motives of the local woodcarvers
are the 'gadzik' ('gad' means reptile), a rythmically waving

A ZAKOPANE COTTAGE OF UNORTHODOX DESIGN

line, the 'leluja', being a conventionalized version of the Turk's cap lily (*lilium Martagon*), the similarly conventionalized silver thistle (*Carlina acaulis*) and the Edelweiss, though this latter is a later addition, due to Austrian influences. A more complicated ornament—the 'parzenica', which may be described as a somewhat extended heart with one or two 'eyes' in its broader part, as in a peacock's feather, and various geometrical motives as further embellishments. It lends itself less easily to a woodcarver's knife or hatchet (the Gurals use small hatchets with great skill for all kinds of wood work), but it frequently adorns the central beam supporting the ceiling, while it appears on most local embroideries, brass brooches, belt clasps, etc.

The Gurals are great artists in wood carving. Their hatchetsticks ('ciupaga'), spoon racks, drinking cups, pails, cheese moulds, chairs and other objects of domestic use, made of wood, are richly, but not excessively, decorated. The delicate and tasteful simplicity of the ornament gives them a pleasant, old-time charm, and it must be regretted that cheap manufactured furniture tends to spoil the local style and makes competition difficult to the peasant craftsman.

The ingenuity of the Gural carpenters was such that they contrived to make complicated door locks, which were opened with a wooden key, without a single metal part. Such locks can still be found in many old cottages, particularly in the villages some distance from Zakopane. Houses also used to be built entirely of wood, wooden plugs being cleverly substituted for nails.

Much in the local wood work vividly recalls Scandinavian patterns, which may or may not be due to the similarities of climate and material (fir wood), though original motives must have been common to the whole of northern Europe, even if they have disappeared elsewhere. Other elements of Gural ornamentation can be easily traced back to Hungarian influences, as the robbers had frequent contact with Hungary during their southern forays.

Wayside shrines furnish another tasteful example of the local wood-carving art. The most typical figure in them is the so-called 'Sorrowing Christ', represented in a sitting posture with his thorn-crowned head supported on a fist. Beehives are also of considerable interest. They are made in the shape of a bishop, a monk or a bear, with an entrance for the bees in the pit of the stomach. When it is an ecclesiastic personality, its folded arms holding the breviary are used by the bees as a sort of bridge to reach the entrance.

Apart from wood carving, glass painting is another, if half-forgotten, local art. The painting, representing usually a holy scene, Virgin Mary, or dancing robbers in red ceremonial head-gear jumping over a bonfire, is made, so to say, in reverse per-spective on the back of the pane; the finer detail is painted first and then comes the background.

Painting on glass on these lines has been recently revived by some sophisticated painters of Gural descent and notably by M. Gąsiennica-Szostak, whose glass pictures have had considerable success.

The Tatra Museum in Zakopane contains an extensive col-lection illustrating Gural folklore—wood objects, arms, cos-tumes, pottery, etc., while the School of Wood Crafts, situated next door to it, has for one of its objects to preserve old traditions and to adapt them to the requirements of modern life.

9

IN A 'HALA'

SHEEP AND CATTLE form the main wealth of the population of the Tatra. As the snow melts on the grazing grounds—or 'hale' (plural of 'hala'), there is a great exodus of sheep flocks to their pastures. This is quite a ceremonial occasion, called 'kierdele', a sort of informal celebration of the advent of the spring. In the autumn a similar migration takes place in the opposite direction.

A hala is a grazing ground owned jointly by a group of villages, who have shares in it which give them the right to keep there so many 'tails' of sheep or cattle each; the shares are therefore called 'tails'. Normally there is no marked boundary between the hale, which form geographical entities, divided from each other by mountains or forests, while surrounding peaks are regarded as a sort of appendix to a hala and in most cases are named after it. None the less, poaching is not infrequent and leads to bitter quarrels and hot-tempered fights.

This system of joint ownership led to considerable legal difficulties when the Polish Tatra Society sought to purchase sites for tourist huts. The Gurals were quite ready to sell their 'tails', but refused outright to part with any definite portion of their common property. It needed much ingenuity to satisfy both sides.

A head shepherd, who is called 'baca' ('c' as 'ts'), is in charge of a whole hala on behalf of its collective proprietors, who entrust to him the maintenance of their flocks, the manufacture and partly the sale of sheep-cheese and milk and such other things as may pertain to the business. At the end of the grazing season the

IN A HALA

baca gives an account of his administration and hands to each particular owner his share of cheese or money, if any has been obtained from its sale.

Every day the average yield of milk is noted and this supplies the basis on which the weight of cheese due to each particular owner is calculated.

The 'baca' is naturally a very important person, and, as the mark of his rank, he wears a leather belt about fifteen inches wide and studded with brass tacks—at least he can wear it when he feels so disposed. Under him are a number of young shepherds—the 'juhas' (yoohas) and some boy apprentices, called 'gońce' (gontse—the n has a soft sound) or messengers. Girls are never employed with sheep, which is a man's job, though it is considered proper that they should milk the cows, when there are any in a hala.

The baca and his staff live in primitive wooden chalets, which only seldom have a fireplace, except in the so-called winter hale, which are not entirely abandoned at the end of the grazing season. The Gural chalets differ in form from the Alpine type, as their roofs are steep on two sides. If there are cows, the chalet is divided into a living room and a cow-shed with a wall between them. Sheep are kept in open sheep folds where they are driven shortly before dusk.

A 'vatra' (fire) is made in the middle of the living room and a cheese kettle is placed over it on an iron tripod. As a rule there is no ceiling and no chimney, so that the smoke from the fire has no proper outlet and escapes through the roof, performing on its way the task of smoking the cheeses which are festooned on the side beams of the roof racks.

Loaves of cheese are made in wooden moulds, often shaped like a conventional cock or sheep, but mostly they emerge from these in a form which can be described as two cones joined at their bases by an ornamental girdle.

The 'juhas' sleep on the floor of the chalet, which is sometimes covered with hay or spruce branches, but is often quite bare,

Whenever the size of the chalet permits they lie down in a star pattern with their feet to the fire. In many chalets, however, sleeping berths are made on shelves below the roof. The shepherds' food is very frugal and consists mainly of a sort of buttermilk—what is left of sheep milk after cheese has been made of it—oat-cake, potatoes and, occasionally, cheese. Meat is a very rare addition to the bill of fare.

No description of a hala would be complete, without mentioning the sheepdogs. These are splendid white beasts, resembling the St. Bernard breed, not much smaller, but of rather heavier build. As they are often kept on a chain, they are liable to become quite angry and even dangerous. Not that it is in the least their nature to be so, and if well-treated, a Liptok, which is the name of the race, is the most good-natured 'white bear' one can imagine. But it is thought, probably not entirely without justification, that a sheepdog is no good if he is not irritable. So, they've just got to be like that. Black gums are considered as a guarantee of this particular quality, and dogs with such gums are much sought after.

Anyhow, it is a great tragedy for a juhas when his grows up placid and refuses to bark, and there is even a funny story about a juhas who tried to teach his dog barking, but it is a little too long to be told here.

WHEN EVENING FALLS: A SHEEPFOLD IN THE FIVE POLISH LAKES

10

WHERE 'IT LIGHTENS O'ER TATRA'

WITHOUT FIGURES of the exact acreage, it may be said that the mountains of Tatra belong in equal parts to the Poles and the Slovaks. They are, as it were, 'sacred' national mountains for both and were meant to become a Polish-Czecho-slovak park of nature. Historical disturbances have for the time being frustrated this project, but it will certainly be revived in the future, since the Tatra has always been not so much a for-midable physical barrier, which its geography might suggest, as a uniting link between the two peoples.

For the Slovak the Tatra is a symbol of his country. On a clear day it can be seen practically from any summit of Slovakia, which it dominates, and it forms the central theme of the Slovak National Anthem, Nad Tatrou sa blýska—

> It lightens o'er Tatra and mighty thunders beat,
> It lightens o'er Tatra and mighty thunders beat.
> Only wait, oh brothers,
> For *they* shall not last,
> And Slovaks will revive!

It is perhaps not a strikingly good rendering of the text, but it is fairly exact, and that is important, for the song has a story to tell. It is a haunting story of oppression and hope. The Slovak looks at his mountains as a thunderstorm roars and grumbles among their granite peaks and flashes of lightning outline their ridges. In the fury of nature he seems to see a reflection of his own feelings and also a promise—only wait, he will be free, his people which has lain prostrate for ages will arise to live again. But he is afraid to speak his thoughts aloud, for a Magyar gendarme in a plumed hat is hovering within earshot. He dare not mention his enemies by name—they are just *they*. They shall not last.

The Slovaks lost their independence almost before it had begun. Strictly speaking there is no tradition of independent Slovakia, though there is a Czechoslovak tradition. For a brief spell of twenty-four years in the dark age of the ninth century, Slovakia united with the Czech country of Moravia into what might be considered as the first Czechoslovakia under the rule of Prince, or rather King, Svatopluk, and rose to great prosperity and considerable power. But this Kingdom of Great Moravia, as it was called, did not last (870–894 A.D.) and in 895 it was overrun by the wild hordes of Arpad. Its cities and churches were looted, such notables as had not made good their escape to Poland or Bohemia or had failed to fall on the battlefield were murdered, and the population plunged into darkness and slavery. Gradually the Arpad Hungarians began to assimilate Western ways, but for the Slovaks the change did not mean much; instead of being Oriental slaves they became feudal serfs. The alien overlords, however, did not bother to impose their own language on the illiterate peasant and the old Slavonic tongue continued to linger, as also did the hatred of the foreign invader, though it could hardly be called national consciousness.

Reformation gave it a fresh impulse. It was characteristic of those times to seek religious expression for political grievances. The Czechs lent a hand. Czech religious propagandists distributed tracts among the Slovak people. These tracts were written in Czech, for it was argued that common people must be approached in their own tongue, and the difference between Czech and Slovak was so insignificant that they could be with justice considered as two dialects of the same language.

E

When John Hus had been burnt alive and his followers defeated, some of them, driven away from their native land, came to settle in Slovakia and even now south of Poprád in the Liptov Valley one encounters peasants who bear old Czech noble names, like Křízka or Jiskra. And old tombstones with Czech inscriptions bear witness to the stormy past.

However, there was no one to collect the threads of old tradition, and, though some Slovaks used to study at the Prague university as far back as the fourteenth century, most of the people remained unenlightened peasants. There was practically no educated Slovak middle class; the large landowners were Magyars or Magyarized Germans and Slovaks. The bureaucracy was also Magyar or completely Magyarized. There was, however, a living Slovak tradition of the Tatra robbers and their chief Janošík (the Polish spelling is Janosik) as the embodiment of the spirit of resistance to feudal oppression.

Only in the nineteenth century came a revival of Slovak tradition and national consciousness, stimulated by the contemporary great Czech movement initiated by František Palacký and others, and whose main Slovak protagonist was the historian Pavel Josef Šafařík. Still, even if the Slovak national movement was not exactly weak, it lacked direction and the Slovaks, as it were, were taken in tow by the Czechs. The Great War of 1914–18 brought liberation and in 1918 the Czechs and Slovaks were united in the single State of Czechoslovakia under the presidency of T. G. Masarýk.

This bit of history, apart from its interest by itself, will serve to explain certain characteristics of the southern side of the Tatra. The Gurals of the North, in their mountain fastness, have preserved intact their old tradition of independence and freedom from serfdom, and though they share the robber stories and their Chief Janošík with the Slovaks, these are with them more of a fact and less of a myth than on the southern side. The lowland Polish intelligentsia, who were enjoying a measure of civic and cultural liberty under the Habsburg rule, elevated the robber

AN INTERESTING EXAMPLE OF SLOVAK BUILDING ART

tradition after the 'discovery' of Zakopane to the dignity of a national cult. Thus, Zakopane for all its development has remained distinctly Polish and local. Not so with Slovakia. The Slovaks were subjected to the uncompromising yoke of Magyar feudal nobility who cared little or less than little for their regional characteristics, culture, building style or song.

The Hungarians had lots of money and soon discovered the possibilities of the Tatra for tourist and health resorts. In the first decade of the present century several such resorts were planned on the northern slopes of the Liptov Valley at the foot of the Tatra. These were small, sumptuous affairs, from the very outset conceived for tourists—mainly rich tourists recruited from the ranks of Magyar nobility. What, however, was gained in comfort was lost in style and the final effect was intensely cosmopolitan in the Austro-Hungarian interpretation of the word. There was a lavish profusion of alien and not infrequently moderately ugly 'Selfridge' and 'Jägerpalast' architecture. Most of these establishments were subsequently bought out by the Hungarian government and then passed into the hands of the Czechoslovak State. There has been no neglect or backwardness and the management has been in every respect good. Buildings constructed under the new regime are in general much pleasanter to the eye than the early Hungarian outcrop, but the original character of the places has not changed very much, and they have suffered not a little from the excessive stress laid on their development for tourists. There are rather too many first-class roads of all kinds, and also marked paths, with benches, inscriptions in four languages, 'televiews' and similar 'civilized' institutions. But, in all fairness it should be stated that the recent development of Zakopane followed much the same lines.

One of the most attractive resorts of the southern side is Štrbské Pleso (Csorba Lake) (see p. 117), situated by the lake of the same name. It is a small place. Two big hotels, a cluster of smaller buildings, restaurants, shops, two railway stations and—a lake. A mountain railway connects the place with Štrba in the

POPRADSKÉ PLESO
LAKE AND HUT

Liptov Valley and a 'panoramic' electric railway starts from
Štrbské Pleso on an easterly course all along the foot of the High
Tatra. Vyšné Hágy, a pleasant settlement nearby, is even smaller,
Tatranská Polianka, Smokovec and Tatranská Lomnica, the
eastern terminus of the Panoramic Railway, Matliary and Belanské Kúpele, the latter at the entrance to the famous Belan Grottoes
with stalactites, stalagmites, electric lighting, guided tours and
admission fees, complete the list.

All these places are rather tiny and spick-and-span as compared
with the sprawling, heterogeneous Zakopane, while the 'real',
old historical townships lie somewhat farther down in the valley
and are not tourist resorts in the proper meaning of the word.
Kežmarok, Velká Lomnica, Štrba, Važec and Liptovský Sváty
Mikuláš are the most important sub-Tatran settlements, which
correspond to places like Nowy Targ on the Polish side.

Among the resorts—Smokovec (Šmeks), situated roughly at
the foot of Gerlach (Gerlachovský Štít), the highest peak of the
group, is probably the most fashionable; it is rather gaudy and
certainly the most 'Alpine' of all. In fact, it is a good starting
point for tours in the rocky central part of the mountains.
Tatranská Lomnica is quiet and pleasantly lost among the trees.
A funicular connects the place with the summit of Lomnica
(Lomnický Štít), the second highest point of the Tatra.

So much for the resorts.

The population of the Slovak side, as one would expect, is
predominantly Slovak. There are also some Czechs and a
sprinkling of Magyar and German (Zips or Spiš) minorities, who
are very apparent in the resorts, but less so when we move a little
farther away from the mountains. In the frontier region between
Poland and Czechoslovakia there are a few Gural villages, such
as Zdiar and Javorina in the North-Eastern Tatra.

Slovak is a language very similar to Czech. In fact, the differences between the two are almost insignificant and normally
would not justify a subdivision into two separate tongues.
Polish is a leap farther off, but not so far from either as to make

VIEW FROM THE SUMMIT OF RYSY
IN THE DIRECTION OF LODOWY

understanding difficult. I have heard the Poles often say that Slovak was easier to understand for them, which may be true, and that, therefore, it was more similar to Polish than Czech. But my own observation would hardly bear out this view. Czech and Polish, on which incidentally the former has exercised at one time a strong influence, belong jointly to the Western Slavonic group, while Slovak displays some characteristic of the Eastern group and occasionally resembles Ruthenian (Red Russian) dialects.

Within the Czechoslovak Republic before 15th March, 1939 there was a certain amount of friction between the Czechs and some Slovak elements, which was largely due to the differences in the economic development of the two component parts. The mainly rural, agricultural Slovakia was in her development a step behind the industrial and urban Bohemia. The Czechs were the more active of the two peoples and their natural economic preponderance gave rise to grievances, whether justified or not, among some sections of the Slovak population. These grievances were fomented and nurtured by foreign propaganda hostile to the Czechoslovak State. Father Andrej Hlinka was the chief exponent of the Slovak Nationalist movement, but he himself never aimed at severing the connection with the Czechs, though he favoured an increased measure of autonomy, somewhat like a similar trend of thought in Scotland.

After his death, his successors lent ear to foreign agitators, who had other objects than Slovaks' welfare in mind. Lack of political experience and some fifth-columnists, such as the present 'premier' Tuka, Mach and Tiso, brought about the disruption of the Republic, already mutilated by the Munich agreement, and the speedy end of both Czech and Slovak independence. Of course, the Slovaks were soon wise after the event, but 'their wrath was wreaked, the deed was done, and now they could go, but they could not go alone'. Slovakia became a Nazi base for the attack on Poland.

AN OLD SLOVAK BAG-PIPE PLAYER

SLOVAK PEASANT WOMEN

II

SLOVAK FOLKLORE

AS WE HAVE ALREADY SEEN, the Slovaks of the sub-Tatran valleys and the Gurals of the Rocky Highlands had one thing in common. They both fought against feudal oppression, which for the Slovaks coincided with national oppression as well. They had in common the Robbers and their legendary chief Janosik or Janošík (Yanoshik), as he is called in Slovakia. The Gurals maintain that Janošík was a Gural and the Slovaks that he was a Slovak, and it is not to be at variance with the truth to assume that they are both right, since at the time when he lived—if ever—there was no clear distinction between them —they were just 'local' and robbers, and national differences as is well known, are apt to be disregarded among men of exalted calling.

Slovak stories and songs about Janošík and his gallant comrades, though in general concurrent with the Gural versions, are not necessarily identical in details. They all, however, agree on one point—he was a hero and a protector of the poor, who used to deal out his wealth to the needy on a generous principle 'from beech tree to beech tree' (od buka do buka). No wonder the Imperial but feminine heart of Maria Theresa fell for his charm.

So, both the Slovaks and the Gurals sing brave songs about their Robber Chief, and if they occasionally contradict each other in some particulars who will take them to task? Many of the songs are common to both sides of the Tatra and it is not unfair to assume that most have originated south of the mountains. In

SLOVAK NATIONAL COSTUMES SOUTH OF THE TATRA, THOUGH SIMILAR TO THOSE
WORN BY THE GURALS, DIFFER IN THE INTERPRETATION OF THE TRADITION

SLOVAK CHILDREN FROM THE TATRA DISTRICT IN NATIONAL COSTUMES

general, however, the Slovaks are somewhat more sentimental than their harder and fiercer northern neighbours in the high Rocky Highlands.

Certainly a song like:

> Through the green rye, through the green rye
> Water's flowing.
> What does my beloved, my beloved,
> What does my beloved say to that?

is Slovak, as it evokes a mood too tender for an average Gural heart.

There is also a similarity of customs and dress. The same ornamental motives are used on both sides of the mountains, though with somewhat different interpretation, but as we move south Hungarian influences become more and more apparent and the similarities become difficult to trace. Whatever the weather, Slovaks in sub-Tatran regions wear white, thick-woven woollen trousers, which they call 'chološne'. They are like those worn by the Gurals, but the design on them is different. It consists of loose, cobwebby lines and the pattern on the side of the trouser leg is in red wool. Also their shirts are not plain white, but embroidered. Young boys wear very short shirts, reaching just below the pit of the stomach, and so attired defy even severe winters. They also wear fur jerkins and a jacket of white woollen cloth, called 'kabanica' (kabaneetsa) and corresponding to the Gural 'cuha'. Most characteristic, and extremely unhealthy, is the huge brass brooch, all hand-wrought with ornamental 'parzenicas', which Slovak boys wear as a collar clasp on their shirt, with the result that the martyr to man's vanity can hardly move his head. Slovak headgear is different from the Gural. True, it is still the same dark-brown or black felt, but the brim of the hat is curled up and either excessively small or excessively large, nothing in between being tolerated by custom. Also it has no string of mussel-shells on the crown.

SLOVAK NATIONAL COSTUMES
IN THE TATRA DISTRICT

On their feet they wear sandals similar to those used by Gurals ('kierpce' in Gural, 'krpce' in Slovak), and the wide Robber's Belt is likewise to be found in Slovakia, where it denotes a married man. But a single fellow must content himself with an ordinary narrow girdle, for which he tries to make up by an elaborately adorned brass clasp. There is in Slovakia no hatchet stick and Slovak shepherds as a rule carry long staffs, similar to the so-called 'Alpenstock'.

The costume of a Slovak girl in the Tatra region differs even more from the Gural dress than the man's. First, she doesn't wear sandals, but special, semi-high-heel boots with a hard leg. The richer or the more attractive the girl the more brass tacks she has on the back side of her boots or 'čižmý' (cheezhmi), as they are called. When young, she wears very short skirts, reaching barely to the knee, but what is lost in length is amply rewarded in number, and several skirts are worn one on top of the other till the poor child is fairly padded out and can hardly sit down.

Another indignity to which a young woman is subjected is the wearing of two pigtails which end with large cockades and lend themselves admirably to being pulled by boys. When a girl appears with pigtails, it means she is a maiden and not engaged to be married—shame on her! Small wonder, therefore, that Slovak girls are in a hurry to get rid of their pigtails, and as soon as they give birth to a child, which is by no means an uncommon occurrence, or, otherwise, become betrothed, they cease to wear them and pleat their hair at the back of their head into the shape of a mussel-shell, called 'chochol' (hohol).

The wedding is a ceremony of old and traditional intricacy performed on similar lines on both sides of the Tatra. In Slovakia the bride on the nuptial evening sits before an open window, wrapped in meditation, while her girl-friends serenade her with the song.

There's a hay-stack standing out in the green meadow
There's a hay-stack standing out in the green meadow.
To-day you're a maiden, To-morrow you'll be wife.

and she, if she still wears her pigtails, bursts into tears and goes on sobbing till the day dies out.

There are also many other old customs, largely dating from pagan times, such as the ceremony of welcoming the renascent life in spring with songs and dances, which corresponds to the old English Maypole festivities.

Slovak peasant architecture is in many ways similar to the Gural, but it is less stern in character—in harmony with the gentler southerly nature of the country. East and west of the Tatra no clear boundary line can be drawn between the Slovaks and the Gurals and both their languages and customs merge into one another almost imperceptibly.

SLOVAK VILLAGE GIRLS CELEBRATE
THE COMING OF THE SPRING

12

CLIMBING

CLIMBING is one of the sports of the place.
The rugged daintiness of the Tatra skyline, its long toothed arêtes, abrupt mountain faces, high and narrow gaps cutting in between pinnacles of solid granite, all look promising to a rock-climber's eye. The small area of the mountains and the number of huts per square mile place most of the desirable objectives within easy reach, which is, of course, a great help when time is short and weather changes quickly, as it often does in the mountain regions.

And these appearances are not deceitful. The Tatra, and the High Tatra in particular, abounds in magnificent climbing, often of great technical difficulty, though the difficulties are mainly concentrated in short stretches. The arêtes of the Tatra probably deserve special mention. Very varied, with cuts and bumps and gendarmes of every imaginable gradient and shape, for the most part of solid, black granulated granite, they give ample opportunities for pleasant exercise,

WHERE NEXT ?
OSTRY, S. FACE

ranging from mere ropeless walks to most exacting 'rock work'. As the average altitude of the ridge above the bed of the valley is between one and three thousand feet, the steepness of the mountain faces below often makes the traverse of a Tatra peak quite an exciting enterprise.

For face ascents the Tatra with its lower altitude cannot approach the sterner Alpine standards. However, it would be a mistake to speak lightly of the Tatra faces. Their rocky part seldom exceeds 2,000 feet. But what they lack in height they can easily make up for in sensation. In fact, many rocks seem to rise at right angles to the valley or even to overhang it, while an inexperienced eye sees only huge polished slabs of smooth stone and sheer black

SCRAMBLING UP THE SLABS ON THE N.W. FACE OF SWINNICA

buttresses, promising a terrifying glissade to certain death for anyone foolish enough to try to climb them. In reality, of course, rocks, even in the Tatra, are seldom perpendicular, let alone overhanging, and in most cases there is an abundance of good holds which make them far less inaccessible than one might expect.

Rock is mostly quite sound, particularly on the south faces, where are most of the popular 'sensational' routes. But north sides, more exposed as they are to snow and wet winds, are frequently weathered and breachy, while some gaps and couloirs below them are apt to display an unpleasant, red–green, papery variety of squashed granite.

F
81

Among the 'horror' routes with good, solid rock, mention must be made of the south face of Zamarla Turnia (Dead Crag) —easiest approach from the Five Polish Lakes or from Hala Gąsiennicowa,* crossing the pass of Zawrat (2,157 m.). The peak itself is inconspicuous, but it falls to the south with some 1,000 feet of sheer rock—a most terrifying sight at close quarters, especially from above and a little aslant. The Eagle Path (Orla Perć) in the same locality is a ropeless ridge tour (chains, fixed ropes, a couple of ladders, etc.) with a few thrills within reach of every able-bodied man or woman and children over twelve. The arête of Kościelec (2,159 m.) nearby is a pleasant climb of moderate difficulty. The surroundings of the famous beauty spot of Morskie Oko (Eye of the Sea) present many climbing possibilities within a few hours' walk from the hotel. On the Slovak side, the hut at Zelene Pleso (Green Lake) is a good starting point for quite exciting climbing tours on the lofty peaks in the immediate vicinity. Also Zbojnická Chata (Robbers' Hut) and Tery Hut belong to the famous climbing headquarters.

Though they are quite impressive, the limestone faces of the east Western Tatra, as in the case of Gewont or Czerwone Wierchy (Red Peaks), are somehow out of favour with the Tatra climbers. This, however, does not necessarily mean that they are wholly undeserving of mention. In fact, I can assure you from personal experience that limestone Tatra routes are often as exacting as the most 'sensational' granite ascents, if not more so.

The upper parts of the West Tatra peaks are, however, easily accessible and provide entertaining panoramic tours, the only danger being that of missing the way if a sudden fog comes up from the valley.

All the most important tourist tracks are marked with oil-painted direction marks—white-colour-white. In dangerous places iron chains and bars have been placed and there are even some iron ladders welded into very precipitous rocks. Such famous sights as the lake of Morskie Oko (Sea Eye) and the

* Caterpillar Alp.

THE ROCKS OF WIDLY (VIDLÝ) FROM
THE S. FACE OF CZARNY SZCZYT (KARFUNKELTURM)

picturesque limestone valley of Kościeliska are accessible by motor road from Zakopane. Finally, apart from the already mentioned téléférique to Kasprowy, another similar mechanical arrangement on the Slovak side of the frontier brings tourists to the top of Lomnica, the second highest peak of the Tatra, where they can admire a vast panorama of rock and cloud.

There were a number of good guides on both sides of the mountains and the local headquarters of the mountaineering clubs could give full particulars to those interested; it is to be hoped that these conditions will be established when the war is over.

Mountaineering in the Tatra may be said to date back to Dr. Chalubiński who was the first to reach most of the easier virgin summits and passes, although some climbing was done also before his times. Among this the first ascent in 1843 of Lodowy (2,630 m.), the third highest peak of mountains, by the founder of the Alpine Club, John Ball, deserves special mention.* The real Alpine exploration of the Tatra, however, began somewhat later when some Alpinists, including Miss Beatrice Thomasson (1899), visited the Tatra and performed there a number of spectacular ascents. Prominent among these Alpinists was a German, Häberlein, who climbed the south face of Ostry (see p. 80). This greatly stimulated the development of Polish and Hungarian rock climbing (Slovakia formed at that time part of the Kingdom of Hungary and most of its upper classes were Magyars or Magyarized Slovaks). Among the Poles, Swierz, Chmielewski, Humpola, Kordys and among the Hungarians, Komarnicky, Rokfalussy and others brought the climbing technique to a high standard already before the last war. The new and daring achievements after the war were closely connected with a group of young enthusiasts who in 1924 formed in Cracow the Tatra Branch of the Polish Academic Sports Association. Later similar organizations were set up in Warsaw and other Polish university cities. For instance, Wieslaw Stanislawski devoted his life to the

---

* Other British mountaineers to visit the Tatra were Leslie and Stephen Bryce, who in 1878 made a few ascents of minor importance.

'solution of difficult rock problems' of the Tatra, and had many fine new routes to his credit before his death in an accident on an expedition which should not have offered great difficulties.

Slovak and Czech climbers in the 'twenties showed little originality and mainly contented themselves with repetitions of old ascents; they also displayed an inclination to excessive indulgence in the *piton-and-karabiner* technique. But during the years preceding the Second German World War the Slovak climbing club JAMES reached a remarkable standard of performance, which strangely coincided with a certain decline in Polish climbing achievement. In fact, the Poles seemed to have decided (some of them were quite positive on the matter) that there was little or nothing to do in their native Tatra and transferred their activities to the more sensational mountains of the Caucasus, High Atlas, Andes and Ruwenzori, the Alps and the Arctic Svalbard. A number of Polish Alpine expeditions had visited these in recent years, some obtaining quite remarkable results (like the first ascent of Cerro Mercedario in the Andes, first ascents in the High Atlas, etc.), and shortly before the war—the Garhwal Himalaya was explored by a small Polish party who met with an avalanche disaster after their successful attack on the eastern summit of Nanda Devi. But even in the Tatra the Poles retained the lead in winter mountaineering and had several fine exploits to their credit (Korosadowicz, Staszel).

The Tatra is little known to British climbers, though in the later 'thirties of the twentieth century it was visited on several occasions by British parties and descriptive accounts have been published in *The Alpine Journal* and other British technical periodicals.

In 1937 Miss Ruth Hale, an English climber who had made the Tatra her favourite mountains, was killed in an accident on the fairly easy but breachy N.W. face of Cubryna, where she was climbing unroped with two Polish companions. She found a resting place at the small dissenter's graveyard of Zakopane.

13

S K I

NO MOUNTAINS can have escaped ski-ing, nor was the Tatra an exception.

The use of this remarkable implement of rapid movement on snow was foreign to the place up to the 'eighties of the last century, though in parts of Poland records of ski-ing reach far back into the historical and probably prehistorical past. Anyhow, it is quite certain that the ski were known there in the sixteenth century and were even used by King Stefan Batory in his campaigns against the Muscovites, while the Swedes, who invaded Poland on two occasions, were also equipped with ski, of which they had left behind a few specimens. Doubtless these excited wild astonishment among the peasants of the Polish plains and were regarded with proper awe as help given to the heretics by the devil. Some bolder spirits, however, sought to imitate the trick and made similar objects of their own, which commend themselves to the modern skier's attention not so much for their perfection as for their curious shapes—some in the collection (now presumably in Germany) of the Warsaw Ethnographic Museum are short, triangular planks which were fastened to the foot with strings.

The new ski-ing, however, came to Poland from the Alps more particularly, and from Austria. The first ski meet was held in the Carpathians (Slavsko) in 1908. People then used big single ski sticks without a disk and braked with these furiously to reduce their speed.

THE VALLEY OF ROZTOKA, IN DEEP WINTER, IS STILL AND SOFT;
NOTHING STIRS IN THE FROZEN AIR

At that time a single ski was called in Polish 'ski' and the plural form of the noun was 'skije' (pr. skeeyē), but now it is known under a Finn name 'narta'. This was considered preferable to the Scandinavian borrowing and has held the ground even against the Slavic 'lizhe', though 'narta' in Finnish meant only 'sledge'. This must remain a puzzle for future philologists, if they ever try to solve it.

However, in 1919, the Polish Ski Association was founded and it became very energetic in fostering ski-ing in Poland, in which it was joined in 1932 by the Polish Society for Promotion of Ski-ing, run on the similar lines to its Scandinavian prototypes. Both these organizations have been dissolved by the German authorities of occupation. But in 1939, shortly before the war, ski-ing was extremely popular in Poland and it was estimated that there were as many as 500,000 skiers there, while the Polish Ski Association alone had 27,000 active members.

Though Poland had many ski-ing grounds, Zakopane was *the* place.* It was larger, closer at hand than other resorts and nothing could rival the glory of the Tatra.

This glory is, however, somewhat double-edged for a skier, as most of the Tatra passages are difficult and demand considerable skill and often much daring, while 'rabbits' can feel safe only in the flatter valleys, like Hala Gasiennicowa, Pyszna, Kalatówki.

In the neighbourhood of Zakopane itself there are numerous 'nursery slopes' where those younger in age or ski-ing proficiency, find safety in numbers. The cable-railway leading from Zakopane to the summit of Gubalówka (Goobaloofka), a hill

* In Czechoslovakia ski-ing was even more widely practised than in Poland, but the Tatra had played a far less important part in its development in view of the generally mountainous character of the country.

THE END
OF A REST

rising about a thousand feet above the town, gives easy access to an extensive panorama and some not too exacting ski descents. A super-nursery is provided by the 6,234 foot (1,957 metre) Kasprowy Wierch (Kaprovy Vierkh) connected with the valley of Kuźnice (Kuzhneetse) by a téléférique which covers a vertical rise of 2,864 feet in something like twenty minutes. Kasprowy slopes gently on two sides, giving moderately exciting runs between three and five miles in length, while special downhill courses have been hewn through the lower wooded approaches by the Polish Ski Association. On these the one-way traffic regu-

lation serves to relieve the density of skiers per square yard when the season is at its peak.

But my sympathies are with those who do not mind an occasional avalanche or a bump on 'marble crust' with protruding rocks unpleasantly close below. For them, there is a wealth of peaks and passes, roadless and lonely, with snows virgin-white, where one's success or—more likely—failure blazes in sunshine for everybody to see, until the next snowfall or wind obliterates the shameful dots on the winding track.

There are the Five Polish Lakes (hut) with the Pass of Zawrat and the 'dreadful gorge' of Szpiglasowa (Shpeeglasova), the ten-mile nonstop run (when snow is good) from Rohatka after a somewhat weary climb, best from the Slovak side, where the 'Zbojnicka Chata'* (Zboyneetska Khata) provides a welcome

* Freebooters' hut.

half-way rest. Most other ski tours in the High Tatra are real Alpine expeditions.

But the more undulating shapes of the West Tatra present a wide range of possibilities for ski-ing.

There are good ski-ing slopes around Kondratowa Hala, whence a somewhat wearisome but not uninteresting tour across Czerwone Wierchy leads to the head of the Kościeliska Valley. In the upper reaches of the valley there is a hut at Pyszna (Pishnâ) which is a good starting point for trips among the surrounding peaks, which are fairly steep, but mainly grass-grown and thoroughly 'ski-able', although one must take good care of avalanches in a thaw or after a fresh snow-fall. South of Czerwone Wierchy (Chervonë Vierhi—Red Peaks) lies the vast and wild group of Koprovské Kopy and the long and equally wild valley Cicha (Tseehâ). The surroundings of the Chocholowska (Hoholovska) Valley and the rocky group of Rohače (Rohachë) will also give a few thrills to an enterprising skier. It is one of the wildest parts of the Tatra, where bears and trees are thickest. But there is a big modern hut in the Chocholovska and a tourist chalet below the Rohače. A splendid primeval forest stretches for nearly twenty miles west of Rohače, which may well help the imagination to visualize what the Tatra used to look like before the encroachment of civilization.

14

THE TWO FIS'ES

FIS STANDS FOR the Fédération Internationale de Ski in which are united the national ski associations of all important countries. Once a year the FIS held a meeting in some place or other where the best skiers of the world came to compete.

When, after a quarrel over the amateur question, the FIS withdrew from the Winter Olympics, leaving them ski-less, the Ski Championships of the World of the FIS acquired additional splendour. But the FIS antics had been somewhat overdone by the Fascist countries, so that some people came to associate the word FIS with fuss.

Zakopane was privileged in 1929 to be the place of a FIS Meeting. And an important meeting it was, since for the first time its programme included a downhill race championed by the Ski Club of Great Britain as a bold innovation in the old run-and-jump traditional Scandinavian bill-of-fare. A British team appeared for the first time on the snows of the Tatra and the Union Jack fluttered in the breeze and the bright sunshine of Hala Gasiennicowa. The race was a close contest won by a margin of three seconds by a Pole Bronek Czech in front of an Englishman William Bracken.

The British team had had a most cordial reception and were full of praise for Polish hospitality and the mountains of Tatra. Otherwise the 1929 FIS was recorded as the coldest one ever witnessed, as the mercury sank one day during the championships to $-48°$ C ! . . . Since then, however, everybody has grown accustomed to the peculiarities of what is known as the 'FIS weather'.

Ten years later, in February, 1939, a FIS meeting was again held in Zakopane, this time as the official Ski Championships of the World, a sumptuous affair with both Downhill and Slalom at the top of the list. The weather 'fissed' frightfully, changing from Siberian severity to the mildness of an English spring with only a coating of ice on the mountains as a reminder of the real season. The Organizing Committee were sweating and gasping, and the whole enterprise just missed being a complete fiasco. The political atmosphere was also distinctly tense and the first signs of the coming storm could not escape a watchful observer.

Thus, one day the special sub-committee for Alpine competitions was engaged in discussing peacefully which of the racers should be labelled 'first class' and which 'second class' according to the rules of the game. The Norwegian representative stated that the Norwegian team were all 'first class', which was received with sympathetic understanding by everybody except the German representative. The German saw in this a symptom of democratic decadence and challenged the Norwegian's statement, demanding that he should prove it. The Norwegian said simply and truthfully that he had asked the Norwegian racers to which class they belonged and they said they were first class, so that settled the matter. But the German would not listen to 'such nonsense'. The Norwegian became visibly excited and retorted that his compatriots were honest country boys and would not tell lies. Their conversation was further complicated by the fact that the Norwegian spoke English, while the German expressed his views through the

A JUMP TURN

medium of his own language. The incident might have developed into a serious international dispute, had it not been speedily liquidated by other members of the committee who

A 'VICIOUS' SKY; THE THAW IS COMING

succeeded in proving the Norwegian's claim to the German's satisfaction.

It did not, however, end the tension.

The straight race was held in rather difficult conditions on wet snow and ice. The best French skier Allais, who was defending his title of the World Champion in Alpine Combination, had broken a sinew during his training and was thus put out of action. The best Norwegian, Fossum had had a bad fall. The Germans held the field.

I was standing close to the manager of the British team about the middle of the course and watching the red-and-white numbers disappear down the slope amidst general excitement.

'What can we poor civilians do against military training?' he murmured doubtfully, shaking his head.

And indeed his gloomy expectations proved right: the Germans (including Austrians) carried the day. The first Englishman, Palmer-Tomkinson was fifteenth and the best English lady, Miss Isobel Roe—seventh.

This filled the manly chest of the German representative on the Alpine Committee with great pride, and when he made a rather belated appearance at the meeting next day, he found it necessary to excuse himself in the following manner:

THE POLISH JUMPING CHAMPION,
STANISLAW MARUSARZ

'We Germans are a ski-ing power. In reality we should have five votes here, not one ... And England? What is England? For England one vote is enough.'

The British representative smiled, took out his pipe and remarked in his best German:

'But look here, dear Herr L. . . . You've got one Reich, one folk, one Führer—so how do you want to have more than one vote?' The guffaw of laughter drowned the German's embarrassment and he behaved very mildly through the remaining part of the meeting.

The Germans, however, were really very good and no other team could have rivalled their extensive training. Their ranks reinforced through the Anschluss with the best Austrian skiers, they won nearly all the competitions, wresting even the jumping laurels from the Norwegians, though they could not rival their style. (Some time later the Norwegians took a terrible revenge in Holmenkollen with the best German somewhere on the eighteenth place in jumping).

The best Polish jumper, Staszek Marusarz, who had been second in special jumping in the Lahti

AN AUSTRIAN INSTRUCTOR
DEMONSTRATES THE *PARALLEL
SWING* ON THE TATRA SNOW

FIS a year before, was fourth in the combined race-jump event.

The blitz of flags and speeches, receptions and actual sports events had passed, and even snow had fallen deep and fresh on the last day of the FIS, giving a magnificent effect in the beams of coloured searchlights mustered up for the occasion. But the meeting brought Zakopane some permanent improvements: several streets had been modernized, the new cable-railway to Gubalówka had been completed, and the old Ski Jump at Krokiew amplified to a Ski Stadium, where later competitions were held.

Also both the first and the second FIS had had a great influence on the ski-ing style. The 1929 one brought with it the broad Alpine boards and the craze for downhill and slalom. In the months of preparation for the second, the coming big event cast its shadow on the older ways of sliding down the mountain slopes. All became 'swing' —parallel swing, of course, weather permitting. Young and old, fair and unfair, were swinging left and right, as by Austrians taught, and they would stampede you to death if you dared say that their ski were not absolutely parallel when they swung. . . .

Meanwhile the grim clash was drawing near.

A WINTER VIEW OF THE WHITE WATER VALLEY IN THE HIGH TATRA

15

THE FOREST AND ROCK
FLORA

THE TATRA can be divided into several regions according to their altitude and the characteristics of the soil. Zakopane and its surroundings lie on an average at some 2,500 feet above sea level, and this makes them a distinctly Alpine country. The southern slopes of the mountains are much warmer and the Liptov Valley is less elevated, so that there is a sharp climatic contrast between the northern and southern part, though the distance between them is barely twenty miles as the crow flies.

In the Rocky Highlands of the north the short but often very hot summer allows some agriculture, on what may be described as the Scandinavian scale. But the soil is poor and collecting all the stones from a field is quite a strenuous exercise. So that oats, barley and potatoes are practically the only possible crops.

It is a region of beech and spruce forest with some larches, ashes, silver firs and a stray rowan or pine here and there. The yew used to be one of the chief trees of the district, but only very few specimens still survive. The northern foothills of the Tatra or the so-called 'regle', are wooded, and in the autumn when the first frosts come, they present a spectacle of peculiar beauty. The dull copper-red beech-trees and the pale gold larches make the background of spruce and silver fir look almost blue, while the mountain skyline beyond is already white with snow or rime, the grass slopes are hazy red, and the leaves of bearberries have been tinted deep carmine by the night frosts. The sky is clear blue, if a

A SILVER FIR

G

little pale, with hardly a suggestion of a cloud. No wind, no rain—a great, crystal calm: the Tatra autumn is fair and still and only in November, or even later, come the first heavy snows.

Above the upper reach of the spruce (1,400–1,500 m.) is the kingdom of dark-green, twisted mountain scrub-pine (*Pinus montana*), juniper, dwarf willows and the most splendid tree of the Tatra forest—the stone pine, known locally under the name of 'limba'. The 'limba' towers like a giant above the last straggling, wind-worn spruces and the sneaky growth of scrub-pine. It is dark and puffy, one of the most attractive conifers.

But the growth of this tree is very slow and it has its enemies. Its smooth, attractive wood is worm-proof and has been much sought after by cabinet-makers, which accounts for the relative scarcity of the species, though on the slopes of Żabie near Morskie Oko and in the Jarorova Valley there are whole 'limba' forests.

Between the forest region and the rock-garden flora of the summits extend the bright-green, boulder-studded mountain grazing grounds—the 'hale'.

Among the smaller plants are found the usual gentians: the bright-blue spring gentian (*Gentiana verna*) and her lesser sister —*Gentiana nivalis*, the large, darker *Gentiana acaulis* (*Clusii*), the purplish-blue fringed gentian (*Gentiana ciliata*), the weedy *Gentiana punctata* of the granites. The small purplish-red *Gentiana carpathica* is to be found in limestone districts—it is similar to *Gentiana germanica*, but the flowers are even smaller, whiter inside and of a paler hue. On the high granite rocks the greenish-white trumpets of *Gentiana glacialis* (similar to *G. acaulis* but about half its size) replace the Edelweiss of the limestones in company with the bright-yellow stars of the Leopard's-bane groundsel (*Dorronicum Clusii*). But probably the most attractive of all Tatra gentians is the tall willow gentian (*G. asclepiadea*), which grows in great abundance at the brinks and clearings of the lower forests. It appears in two varieties. Some plants grow

WIELKA ŠWISTÓWKA AT THE UPPER LIMIT OF THE SPRUCE

TATRA FOREST

straight with alternate leaves and blue flowers (rather smaller than *G. acaulis*) winding up the stem, which is about two feet in height. Others spread to the sides their elegantly arched stems, with leaves and flowers spaced sideways, flat. This variety is particularly attractive.

The Turk's cap lily (*Lilium Martagon*) is one of the traditional decorative motives ('leluja') as also is the silver thistle (*Carlina acaulis*), very common in the Tatra Highlands. Lady Slipper orchid is rare, but several other orchids, like *Orchis globosa*, *Nigritella angustifolia*, the vanilla-scented, white *Coeloglossum albidum*, and the fragrant orchis (*Gymnadinea odoratissima Rich.*) are very frequent. Dark-mauve gladioli and cotton grass (*Linnea borealis*) are common features of a wet Tatra meadow later in the summer. The spring brings shy soldanellas, the spurge-olive (*Mezereum Daphne*), the fragrant *Pyrola uniflora*, the *Primulae-officinalis* with its faint smell of peaches and, among the dolomitic rocks of the lower valleys, the similar, but smaller, thick-leaved *auricula* with bright, chrome-yellow flowers with an almost overpowering scent. Meanwhile higher up on the green 'hale' the snow is melting and mauve crocuses open up their wax-like chalices. They look lovely against the chaste background of pastel-green grass, patches of snow and the sombre forests, above which rise the snow-covered peaks.

Campanula barbata, C. pusilla and another species of tall plants with huge white and violet flowers are all common in the Tatra, though the latter are confined to the lower regions. The granite flora is not very rich as compared with the exuberance of the limestones, though lime tends to tinge the flowers white and white thyme is very frequent among others. But it has its white cushions of *Androsace* and the pink cushions of moss campion (*Silene acaulis*), the dark-red and yellow *Semperviva*, which in June take the place of the *Saxifragae* of the Low and Belan Tatra. Some grassy slopes in the granite part are covered with the dazzling white of *Anemone alpina* and its minor brother *A. narcissiflora*.

SPRING FLOWERS IN A TATRA FOREST
PRIMULA OFFICINALIS

The dark-blue Common and the light-blue Panicled monks-hood adorn the precipitous limestone walls, while the tall yellow Foxgloves may be found growing in clumps along the gullies of the wooded slopes.

In the Western limestone Tatra I have a valley of my own choosing—it is called Wielka Świstówka. A tourist seldom ventures to this secluded, weird place and a great silence reigns there among the steep walls of weathered stone and the shaggy forest, broken only by the faint sound of a trickling stream, the occasional wail of an eagle, the buzz of a stray bumble-bee or the hiss of a chamois. But what wealth of wild flowers! You will find there almost all the flowers I have mentioned and many others as well. The Alpine rose, the delicately indented *Primula minima,* the scentless yellow *Viola biflora,* the pale-violet *V. calcarata* and the large pink *V. glacialis,* Glacier crowfoot (*Ranunculus glacialis*), and *R. parnassifolius,* the violet, yellow-hearted Alpine aster, mountain flax, Alpine columbine (*Aquilegia alpina*), *Geum montanum, Pedicularis foliosa* and *P. verticillata* and a legion of minor plants and dwarf shrubs. Among the latter the *Dryas octopetala* with its glossy dark-green leaves and attractive eight-petalled white flowers deserves special mention. It came to the Tatra from the Arctic during the Ice Age together with the stone pine, the Carpathian cudweed, the *Arachangelica officinalis* and a tiny crustacean, which lives in two small, isolated tarns in one of the valleys and is otherwise to be found nowhere except northern Scandinavia. They all obviously liked it there, for they stayed behind when the glaciers retired to the North.

But two flowers, perhaps neither large nor very spectacular are my special favourites. One is the Alpine poppy. It is smaller and frailer in the Tatra than its Alpine counterpart, and it is never white, but creamy and has a delicate scent of musk. The plant is so frail that it soon wanes if plucked and loses its fragrance. Another is the *Dianthus Tatrae,* the Tatra carnation. It grows in little clumps, often in small cavities of a rock wall ; the flowers are double, white or light pink and have a pleasant musky smell, stronger than and different from the poppy. Another mountain carnation, which grows in the Tatra and which you may not know, is the *Dianthus glacialis*; it has a largish, plain, odourless, pink flower, sitting on a short stem.

The clothy, grey-blue *Clematis alpina* is rare and among the spruce branches, it easily escapes notice, as the creeper has few leaves which are narrow and wide-spaced.

Both in 'my valley' and in many other limestone sites Edelweiss will be found and that not necessarily on precipitous ground, as the popular fancy would have it. Its local names are 'Szarotka' (*pr.* 'sharotka') or 'Pussyfeet' (Kocie lapki). It would be quite common, in fact, had it been less relentlessly pursued by holiday-makers who have succeeded in nearly exterminating the plant in all easily accessible places.

Whortleberries, bearberries, blackberries and wild straw-berries are found practically everywhere in the Tatra, and if you know where to go and it is the right season you simply can't miss wild raspberries, which, albeit smaller, have a flavour that no garden-grown variety can rival. Redcurrant and gooseberry bushes grow wild on some of the Western Tatra slopes, but they are not so easy to find and often an exacting, if not dangerous, scramble is needed to reach them.

AT THE EDGE OF THE TREE LINE
A STONE PINE, SPRUCES, JUNIPERS AND DWARF PINES

16

ABOUT BEARS, MARMOTS AND SUCHLIKE

THE ONCE RICH FAUNA of the Tatra is largely on the ebb. The wolf is extinct and so are the lynx, the wild cat and the wolverines, though I have heard that some lynxes have survived in the wild woodland of the western part. But there are still about a dozen couples of brown bears (*Ursus Arctos*) roaming among the crags and forests of the Tatra, and if one is fond of berries, though I am not sure whether bears like bearberries, one has a chance of meeting a competitor who may not appreciate one's presence. On the whole, however, bears are quiet, shy creatures and, if not angered, behave politely. But a she-bear with cubs doesn't like to be disturbed in her maternal cares; I have met one myself and never before or since have I climbed so fast on rocks so nearly perpendicular to have a better view of the other side of the mountain.

Of non-carnivorous forest-dwellers the stag would be the most impressive, had not a couple of European bisons been imported into the Tatra by Prince Hohenlohe. Chamois are quite plentiful and of the smaller inoffensive creatures a marmot (*Marmota marmota*) can be often seen basking in sunshine among the scree. He would be quite difficult to notice owing to his grey-brownish fur, which resembles the colour of stones and dry grass. But his shrill whistle by which he warns his comrades of the approaching danger as he scuttles into a burrow can be heard for half a mile around among the stillness of the mountains.

LOOKING DOWN THE GAP OF WAGA (VAHA)

This fat fellow is very curious and if one walks quietly to his burrow and waits for a few minutes he is almost sure to reappear and give one another chance to look at him.

Once I approached to within five yards of a marmot before he ducked into a hole under a boulder. But I sat down close by and started to whistle. In a minute or two the marmot, probably disgusted by my inept performance, poked out his head. I pretended not to notice him, and gradually he grew bolder and crept out altogether, though he did not venture far from the entrance to his burrow. Finally there he sat in his full glory, staring at me with his brown eyes, obviously quite fascinated by his own audacity.

Of the birds the mountain eagle (*Aquila chrysaëtus*) is the most impressive. He is very rapacious and strong—just a little less than a yard from the ground when standing and the span of his wings reaches two yards. In fact he may be quite frightening at close quarters, if one succeeds in approaching him from the lee, hiding behind the rocks; but this is not too likely, for eagles don't enjoy human company and make off straight away at the sight of a tourist.

Less impressive than the mountain eagle, the spotted eagle (*A. clanga*), common in some parts of the British Isles; one species of hawk and one of falcon are also found in the Tatra. Of other big birds the woodcock will be seen sometimes in the Tatra forest.

Among the smaller birds there are many usual mountain inhabitants: the yellow wagtail, the dipper, the wren, the richly-purplish bull-finches pottering about in the snow (a very becoming background), the wonderful Alpine aeronaut—the Mauervogel, who makes a practice of 'power-diving', almost grazing the edge of steep rock buttresses.

Trout live in the lakes and rivulets of the Tatra, while salmon-trout are encountered in the lower waters. There are four species of lizard, including the small graceful *Lacerta vivipara* which doesn't lay eggs but bears tiny, wriggling, dark-brown young and leaves them without much formality to find their

IN THE FALLING RAIN
PRECIPITOUS ROCKS RISE IN DIM OUTLINE
OVER THE WHITE WATER VALLEY

way about in the world. Salamanders are very frequent on the wooded slopes of the lower hills where they nestle in old decayed tree stumps. There are, of course, also frogs—green and grey. The only venomous reptile is the viper. Even this, however, is mercifully rare, and I have never seen one during my ten years' stay in the Tatra.

Those who have a liking for butterflies will see in the high mountain clearings a *Parnassius Apollo* alighting on an Alpine anemone, or, if they are lucky, a *Parnassius Mnemozyne;* the the Camberwell Beauty (*Vanessa Antiope*), the Swallow-tail (*Papillio Machaon*) and *Argynnis Paphia* are other very common species.

All rare animals, as well as plants, are protected.

The caves of the Tatra contain numerous bones of cave-bears (*Ursus Arctos spaeleus*) and smaller extinct animals. Also human remains and some paleolithic tools have been found, but their exact age and relation to other similar European finds have not as yet been sufficiently established.

The Tatra have no mineral riches worth mentioning. But at one time, under the Polish and Hungarian kings (Matthew Korvin Huniadyi), some gold veins of poor content were worked in the sides of Gerlach and Krywań (Krivaň—every mountain in the southern Tatra has four names: a Polish, a Slovak, a German and a Hungarian one, often without any trace of common identity). Also pyrites, iron ore, copper and silver used to be mined about 200–300 years ago. The mines, however, have been long since exhausted and abandoned. Amethysts and garnets are the only precious stones found in the Tatra in very small quantities, far too small for anything like regular exploitation. Mountain crystal is fairly frequent, but most specimens are small and valueless.

There are a few stone quarries, which have somewhat spoiled the view, particularly near Zakopane; even these, however, have been largely abandoned. But the excavations left over by them may be of interest to a geologist, as they disclose the traces of a seashore from the distant time when the Tatra was an island in a mid-European sea. I remember seeing in one place petrified mussel-shells embedded in a rock, which had been uncovered by an explosion of dynamite. Imprints of fern-trees, Calamites (giant Horse-tail), *Lepidodendrons* and suchlike are found occasionally on the Tatra marles, though in limestone Numulites are by far the most frequent fossil.

MARMOT IN PERSON

17

THE SEA EYE AND THE
GOLDEN DUCK

NEARLY ALL THE TATRA LAKES are situated in the central
granite group of the High Tatra. In the limestone regions
of the West and Belan Tatra the soft rock slowly yields to
water, which eats through its upper layers and disappears under-
ground, chiselling out on its way caves and passages, to emerge
again lower down the valley. In other words, one must choose—
lakes or grottoes: to have both at a time is a virtual impossibility.

In fact, there is only one lake of any importance in the limestone part of the West Tatra. It lies at the end of the Kościeliska
Valley, a famous and somewhat too popular beauty spot connected with Zakopane by a highroad of inferior quality. But
even this lake rests in a cavity of igneous rock, though limestone
crags may tower above it in the south. The Belan Tatra is completely lakeless. To make up for this, however, some of the most
spectacular caves—the Belanské Kûpele heading the list—with
stalactites and stalagmites are found in that part of the mountains.

So, the High Tatra is the place for lakes.

Its lower valleys are V-shaped, the usual result of water erosion, prescribed by geology manuals. Dark spruce woods, here
and there gashed by avalanches, climb the steep slopes on both sides
up to the labyrinths of scrub-pine, bright-green cushions of
grass and bear-berries, and the naked rocks of the summits. But
as we move up the valley we usually meet an abrupt step of

THE BLACK LAKE AND THE SEA EYE FROM RYSY

varying height with a waterfall hanging its lace of spray across gloomy, darkened rocks. Sometimes there are several successive steps like that, rising in terraces one after another.

Above the step the valley becomes flatter and broader and spreads fanwise to the sides. It is the end of the water-erosion work. An expert eye will at once notice the regulation U-shaped workmanship of the long-since-vanished glaciers.

It is where the lakes live.

The vanished glaciers have done their work well. They have dredged the rock bed by the pressure of flowing ice into deep cavities and, as if to make sure that the water should not escape, deposited terminal moraines just at the brink of the steep cut, marking the last reach of their power. The brooks from melting snows have duly filled out the cavities with waters, cool and clear, ready to reflect the grim rock walls shooting up steep above the ice-polished grey slabs of granite and the mosaic of debris, grass and pine.

The Tatra lakes are not large—they fit the size of the mountains—but some are quite deep. Thus, one of the 'Black Lakes', Czarny nad Morskiem, is fully 260 feet deep near its centre—more than the average depth of the Baltic Sea—and Wielki Staw or Great Lake in the Five Polish Lakes is 250 feet deep.

The depth of the water and the surroundings make most of the Tatra lakes appear black, or, more exactly, a dark-steely colour, with a touch of blue and violet and green and even a hint of black, though the painters may not believe in the existence of black in nature. Accordingly most of these are called Black Lakes—Czarny Staw, 'czarny' (charni) meaning black and 'staw' (pr. like staff) lake or tarn. But there are also at least two Green Lakes, a White, a Blue and a few Red ones. Another numerous group is that of the 'Frozen Lakes'. In fact, more than one of them, though mostly smallish, lie at something like 7,000 feet, and are consequently completely or partly frozen for the best part of the year.

Many lakes are named after places facing them or otherwise

THE BLACK LAKE OVER THE SEA EYE

H

associated with them. This is particularly the case on the Slovak side of the mountains. Sometimes they are named both for their colour and locality, and this is rather necessary with the Black Lakes, well over a dozen in number. There are also Lower and Upper, Big and Small lakes to fit the circumstances.

But the lake of all the Tatra lakes has been given a name both romantic and unexpected—it is called the Sea Eye*—Morskie Oko (Meerauge). An old superstition would have it that this lake was connected with the Baltic by a subterranean link and that wreckage of sunken ships would be found now and then after a stormy night in its calm waters. One need hardly insist on the absurdity of this belief, which has apparently originated in the discovery of an old, mouldy boat which sank there at some distant date. It may, however, add to the natural beauty of this unique sight, somewhat marred, alas, by an hotel built right on top of the head moraine with its noisy car and cab park close behind it. A highroad winds its way down from the place towards Zakopane and over a bridge to Czechoslovakia.

The Sea Eye is situated relatively low, within the spruce forest region. The stone pines, dark and puffy, by the water edge are silhouetted against the 3,000-feet-high walls of sheer rock which just fail to encircle the lake. About a hundred yards higher up to the east another glacier *cirque* contains a somewhat smaller lake, whose dark waters contrast with the deep aquamarine-green of the Sea Eye. It is the Black Lake over the Sea Eye (Czarny Staw nad Morskiem Okiem, as its full title runs), mentioned above as the deepest lake of the Tatra.

Across the ridge, due west of the Sea Eye, extends the most remarkable congregation of lakes in the Tatra—the squatty and windy, open Valley of the Five Polish Lakes, which include the largest and second deepest of all Tatra lakes, already referred to. The valley falls with a steep cut of some 600 feet into the V-shaped Roztoka†, and a mighty waterfall of Siklawa (w like v),

---

* This appellation was at one time used generically for all mountain lakes.
† See illustration, p. 87.

THE SEA EYE AFTER THE FIRST SNOWFALL

fed by the waters of the lakes, shoots down a jagged gorge in a pall of spray.

The Csorba Lake or Štrbské Pleso (pronounce as you like) lies on an open plateau rising from the Liptov Valley at the foot of the mountains. The lake is hemmed in on three sides by spruce forests and a little, fashionable resort spreads out on its southern shore. It is unique in character, as it is not dwarfed by the nearness of massive peaks and, though smaller than several other Tatra lakes, it would at first sight appear by far the largest of them—a quiet, inoffensive fraud.

In fact, there has been a measure of natural justice in the way in which the frontier between Poland and Czechoslovakia has been drawn, leaving most of the largest lakes on the northern Polish side and most of the highest summits on the southern.

The White Water Valley* (Biala Woda) is probably the most beautiful of the Tatra valleys, though tastes may differ. In any case, it leads towards the chain's highest peak—Gerlach, and the scenery of cathedral-like rocks, rising amphitheatrically over the lakes and forests below, is a piece of perfect 'architecture' of inspiring, airy grandeur. At its head, the valley spreads fanwise, rising by a succession of steep steps to towering mountain walls and narrow, giddy passes. Calm lakes are sheltered in the cavities of these steps. They are not the largest, nor the deepest, but perched high above the wooded valley with a wide horizon beyond, at the foot of precipitous granite buttresses, they borrow from their surroundings what their own nature has denied them.

The Czech Lake and the Duck Lake, whether shining like a sheet of silver through trailing fogs, or resting like bits of sky among rock, pine and grass, with the background of vast mountain vistas paling away in the distance, are full of light and life. Now the breeze will draw a sudden net across their perfect mirrors or a cloud break their blue. The Duck Lake owes its name to a strange legend. It is on its surface that the Golden Duck of the Tatra chooses to reveal herself to mortal eyes, when it suits

* See illustration, p. 95.

ŠTRBSKÉ PLESO (CSORBA LAKE)

her nature. The mortal remains spell-bound by the sight of the fairy bird coming to announce something whose meaning is not clear to the writer, but which must certainly be of great importance.

In reality, when sunshine falls through the rocks above the lake and the fogs come steaming upwards from the valley, they say that sometimes a bright, golden flash of light will show on the water. When one's eyes are tired of exposure, it is a well-known mountain phenomenon that one is apt to see strange things in the dim outlines of the fog. . . . So who knows but the Golden Duck may have actually been seen by some people. I have seen myself crowds of ghosts in the streaming fog after a sleepless bivouac on a mountain face and am quite disposed to believe in the Golden Duck.

But duck or no duck, the Duck Lake is beautiful and it is so restful to lie down in the grass near its water after a strenuous climb and look at its still, downward world.

Incidentally, the caves of the Tatra have a fairy fauna of their own and the King of Snakes with a crown of gold and precious stones on his head used to have among them his subterranean palace. At present, according to the latest information, he seems to have been hospitably received in Loch Ness, where he is living as a refugee. The Sleeping Knights, however, have been too sleepy to move and have certainly stayed in their cave in the Kościeliska Valley.

ONE OF THE "FROZEN LAKES"

DUCK LAKE

18

THE SKY OF THE TATRA

Mountain weather changes often, quickly and unexpectedly and with it changes the aspect of the sky.

> Here comes the rain, here comes the rain,
> > Comes the downpour!
> It will lash and soak, it will lash and soak
> > Fair Janosik's face!

runs one of the songs about the famous Robber Chief.. . . So, the rain will come in torrents of water, with flashes of lightning and the dull roar of thunder, thrown back from summit to summit, from ridge to ridge. It will sweep the mountains, making the rocks dark-purple, the forests almost black and the meadows bright-green and alight with sunshine, reflected in lingering drops of dew on the grass and the spruces. And the sky of the Tatra will be dark, dark blue, as only a mountain sky can be, with white puffy clouds, or it will become once more low, grey and threatening.

Fog is frequent in the Tatra, but it seldom descends as low as the main valley. The play of fog and sunshine on the mountains often lends attractive effects, and sometimes Zakopane and all the deeper valleys vanish under a carpet of mist and the Tatra alone towers above in bright sunlight. When you are on a ridge with fogs drifting across it and the sun stands low, you can see your own shadow projected on the background of fog till it grows enormous, surrounded by a circular rainbow—the so-called

STORM CLOUDS

THUNDERSTORM OVER THE HIGH TATRA

halo, a well-known Alpine phenomenon. There is a superstition that whoever has seen it three times will not meet death in the mountains, and as the phenomenon is not particularly rare this sort of indemnity can be easily acquired. . . .

Sunrise in the Rocky Highlands, owing to their high altitude, is bright pink and the sunrise sky is pale jade-green, while the dark-blue curtain of the night can be seen clearly as it is gradually sinking below the western horizon. Summer thunderstorms bring heavy, creamy cumuli, which blaze with orange at sunset, and wisps of dark violet-grey cloud floating across their piled masses. But the most beautiful effects are produced in the sky by the local variety of the foehn wind—'halny', which is particularly frequent in spring and autumn.

At low atmospheric pressure on the northern side of the mountains, the warm air from the southern side, which knows no foehn, is sucked up by the colder northern valleys. It contains more moisture than the lower temperatures of the northern slopes would permit, and as it rushes across the main chain it is filled on the way with a swirling turmoil of cloud, which pours down from the ridges to break again into separate cloudlets and dissolve a few hundred yards later. The warm breath of the 'halny' sometimes approaches the violence of a tornado, resulting in damage to houses. There is something uplifting in its elemental power. But skiers and people with a bad heart are by no means enthusiastic about it.

In the sky, however, the 'halny' is apt to result in most glorious sunsets with colours which have to be seen to be believed and are presumably due to a fine water dust in the higher layers of the air.

Sometimes the sky is almost purple with lemon-yellow and chrome-yellow clouds, which change to flamboyant orange and brick-red as the sun sinks lower below the horizon. At other times green clouds are set against a sky of clear metallic blue, or again the sky itself becomes green and the clouds purple. Add to this the background of rugged peaks, deep purple or blue, and you can visualize the scene.

SUNSET CLOUDS OVER THE TATRA

SUNRISE FROM THE SUMMIT OF LOMNICA (LOMNICKÝ ŠTIT)

Of course, such sunsets are relatively rare. But their Apocalyptic glory is almost unforgettable. And you can always count on a few that may be perhaps less spectacular, but are quite beautiful.

Alpine glow in the Tatra cannot rival the glories of the Dolomites. All the same, it is quite impressive, especially after rainfall, when moisture on the rocks serves to enhance the effect, or in winter.

A night sky, moonlit or not, in summer and in winter, always has its own charm. The high altitude above the sea and the transparent air make it a sparkling carpet of stars and the Zodiac Light is clearly visible during the summer months.

19

WAR

O N 2ND SEPTEMBER, 1939 it was reported in a telescriptor despatch from Zürich:
'Heavy fighting between exceptionally large forces of both German and Polish troops is in progress in the Carpathians. The fighting was exceptionally bitter in the mountainous parts around Bialka, Jurgów and near the health resort of Zakopane.'

So much for the Press. In actual fact things were somewhat different. Zakopane and the Tatra forming a sort of peninsula protruding into German-occupied Slovakia, the Polish positions there were outflanked, even though the Tatra formed a splendid natural barrier in the south. It was considered therefore unwise to concentrate large forces on this sector, and according to reliable reports Zakopane was held by a single company of the Polish First Highland Regiment who succeeded in keeping at bay for three days the far superior Alpine forces of General List attacking from the south. Some bayonet fighting took place on the main ridge when the Germans forced it at several easier points. Tank attacks were made in the direction of Zakopane across the frontier rivulet of Bialka in the east, and the first of them was beaten back.

One of the tanks was destroyed by a Polish skier Genek Lorek who set it ablaze, but was killed when the tank exploded.

In the end, however, the Poles were completely overwhelmed, despite desperate resistance, and only in the mountains did small detachments continue to hold out for a few days until they ran short of supplies.

The place itself suffered little in the fighting, as there had been no bombing and no artillery bombardment. A few minor incidents followed upon the occupation of the town, but in general it was relatively peaceful and did not exceed what one can expect of the entry of enemy troops into a conquered territory.

One feature, however, deserves special mention.

The attacking troops were apparently led by some of the German skiers who had competed in the previous FIS Championships at Zakopane, which proves beyond a shade of doubt how useful such sporting meetings can be, if only treated from what may be called the 'broader national point of view'!

The tradition of the First Highland Regiment who distinguished themselves in the battles of the September campaign in Poland is now carried on by the Polish Highland Brigade.

The Highland Brigade took part in the operations of the Allied expeditionary force near Narvik, where they contributed to the capture of this iron port by their spirited attack on Bjerkvik and Ankenes. At present the Brigade is stationed in Scotland, where they await another opportunity to prove their valour when the call is made.

20

TEMPORA MUTANTUR, NOS ET MUTAMUR IN ILLIS

SINCE THE OCCUPATION of Poland, Zakopane has been made a rest centre for the members of the Wehrmacht and the new tourist hotel at the Kalatówki Alp has been taken over for Dr. Frank's private residence. The Tatra Society has been dissolved and its property confiscated on behalf of the Karpathenverein, once a German-minority club, and Dr. Ley's *Kraft durch Freude* association. Some Austrian ski instructors, once active on the nursery slopes of the Tatra, have emerged from their larval state and blossomed out in full Gestapo uniform. There have been also some others who have adorned themselves with the mark of the 'double-cross' or 'sudden cross', either to keep away 'suddenness' from themselves or for other motives. The Tatra Highlanders have been proclaimed descendants of the Marco-manni, and, as became the occasion, they accepted the honour with the grave silence of Indian chieftains.

The streets of Zakopane are full of grey uniforms and the illustrated periodicals of the Reich are teeming with illustrated praise for this *urdeutsch* (ancient German) place, recovered—it must be presumed—after 2,000 years of foreign domination . . . at last!

For some time after the fateful date of 15th March, 1939, young men in unkempt green-khaki uniforms used to sneak into Poland across the mountains, looking warily around. Then other young men in the navy-blue uniform of the Slovak

Hlinka Guard followed in their wake—for what good is a country, particularly a small country without a guard? When the Polish campaign was over, the migration changed its direction, though the final destination remained the same. This time it was the young men of Poland who were stealing through the Tatra, south, across Slovakia to Hungary, and thence to France and Britain to join their new national army. Many were killed on their way and Staszek Marusarz, the Polish ski champion, among them. But now this way has been blocked, since the present situation in Hungary can be summed up in the words of an old local ditty,

> Hey Magyar's drinking, hey Magyar's paying,
> Hey, for the Magyar children weep....

Low, grey clouds trail over the spruce tops, water trickles down the rock faces of the Tatra, and the sun and the stars rise and set over them every day....

London, March, 1941.

WHITE-WASHED STONES MARK THE FRONTIER BETWEEN POLAND AND CZECHOSLOVAKIA (P ON THE ONE—ČS ON THE OTHER SIDE)